The Intense Entrepreneur

The Intense Entrepreneur

How to turn your quirks into strengths, to intensify your business

Nikki Petersen

Acute Yeti Books
Boulder, CO

All rights reserved. No part of this publication may be reproduced, distributed, or transmitted in any form or by any means, including photocopying, recording, or other electronic or mechanical methods, without the prior written permission of the publisher, except in the case of brief quotations embodied in critical reviews and certain other noncommercial uses permitted by copyright law.

The Intense Entrepreneur © Nikki Petersen. All Rights Reserved, except where otherwise noted.

Contents

	Praise for The Intense Entrepreneur	vii
	Disclaimer	ix
	Acknowledgements	x
	Introduction	1
1.	What is Intensity?	23
2.	Finding Your Voice	55
3.	Leadership	83
4.	Networking for the Intense Entrepreneur	98

5.	Sales and Marketing	113
6.	Community	138
7.	Iteration and Sustainability	145
8.	Conclusion	151
	Appendix A -- Resources	155
	Appendix B -- Activities	159
	Appendix C -- Lists	164
	About the author	171

Praise for The Intense Entrepreneur

"Though I've read umpteen million books (exaggerating just a bit) on business, Nikki was the first person who I felt was speaking to me as a gifted person who sees the world differently in the context of business opportunities. She's quirky, funny, and so down to earth that you can't help but laugh and learn from her."

— Lisa Epler Swaboda

"In the past, I have struggled with my

intensities and they've slowed down my progress. Nikki's book has helped me to better understand and work with my them so that they actually benefit my business. Unlike many books on business strategy, the information presented in *The Intense Entrepreneur* actually makes sense and is a perfect balance of information and action — action that I took immediately in my own business. Nikki's humor mixed with her ability to present these insights in a straightforward, no nonsense way allowed me to instantly connect to the ideas and concepts. After reading this book, I feel a renewed sense of motivation and have a really doable plan to approach my work as an intense person."

— Amy Schief

Disclaimer

All of the examples included in this book are based my real experiences and those of people in my life. However, in all cases, I have used composite examples and changed names and identifying characteristics to protect the privacy of the individuals. I have adapted examples to more clearly illustrate points.

Acknowledgements

I want to thank everyone who helped me bring this book to fruition. I could have done it without you, but the book would have been messy, ugly, and disorganized. Heck, it might still be, because I sort of suck at taking advice.

I also want to thank Bert, Oscar, and Vera, my biggest fans. You are the best thing to ever happen to me and I am privileged to be your mom. But really, I would be even more thankful if you'd shower more often.

Introduction

Have you ever felt like you've pushed potential customers or clients away because you're "too intense"? Do you feel like you're too quirky to be successful and that no one gets you? It can be isolating and lonely when you can't make the authentic connections you're seeking.

Are you wondering how you'll find enough clients to sustain the lifestyle you dream of with your new business? Maybe you took a job because being an entrepreneur wasn't supporting you financially (but you dread working a nine-to-five or retail job). That leaves you feeling defeated and deflated.

Do you just want to help people, if they could only hear your message? Do you feel like no one understands your big ideas about what you think their business can do? It is utterly depressing and disheartening, to feel that what you have to offer to the world will never be truly felt by anyone besides you.

This book will help you to discover who your tribe is, and how to reach them in a way that speaks their language—and feel the mindset of abundance when that really clicks. You will develop confidence in your authentic message so that you know your big ideas are falling on the right ears. You will be able to recognize, honor, and use your quirks as your business superpowers.

In writing this book, I tried to address and merge two central ideas: intensity and entrepreneurship. I've yet to come across a book that addresses both (if you know of one, let me know!), which is what makes this book unique.

The largest part of the book addresses the easy part—entrepreneurship. There are a plethora of books published today on entrepreneurship. That's nothing new. However, there is definitely a need for a book or resources that address entrepreneurship in the context of being intense, which I will define next.

For the purposes of this book, intensity and giftedness will be used interchangeably. Wait—don't stop reading!! Using the word "intensity" in my title was actually a very difficult decision for me. On one hand, I feel that, because I am addressing giftedness, I should be able to use that term freely on the front cover as well as throughout the book. On the other hand, the general public is put off by the G-word and I am sure that my book would be passed over if the word "gifted" were in the title (and what would be the point of writing it, if I didn't mind that it would be ignored on the shelves?).

One very common reason so many gifted individuals have so much pain, isolation, and depression is because they feel shunned for declaring themselves as gifted, if they're even aware of it. Many unidentified gifted adults dismiss the idea without reading further because they don't believe it could apply to them.

As an example, a close friend of mine dismissed her own giftedness for many months. After discovering her son's giftedness and her husband's giftedness, she finally took a screening test—and her score was 147 (the minimum IQ for to meet the traditional definition of "gifted" is 130). Now, what that means for her is a very personal story, but suffice it to say that the general perception of giftedness is usually pretty distorted.

Although the collection of respectable literature for giftedness and intensity is slowly developing, most authors talking about giftedness often shy away from the subject as it pertains to adults. Being a parent, I fully support advocating for the education of gifted children. As a gifted adult, I shouldn't have to point out that gifted kids grow up to be gifted adults, and you don't grow out of giftedness. In her TED talk, Ash Beckham says that we are all stuck in some sort of closet, and that when we can be ourselves it opens the door. Unfortunately, public approval of the G-word isn't quite where it should be yet, and trying to come out of that closet doesn't always result in acceptance.

As soon as you use the G-word, people change. Their attitudes, demeanor, and body language can all switch to defensive, offensive, and downright rude. I want, so badly, to fight that stigma, like Ash fights the stigma of being shunned for being gay. I also realize that it can't happen overnight and I have to persist. So please be kind, patient, and gentle with yourself and others when hearing or using the G-word—please realize that gifted people are fighting invisible battles, just like everyone else. I hope that you can read on because I truly believe it's worth it.

You may be saying, "But I'm not gifted," or "I was gifted in school, but not now"—or even "I can't be gifted because I was never good in school". Please, please don't let the G-word get you down or put you off this book. If you've ever been told that you're "too intense" or you come on too strong, or if the questions in the first few paragraphs felt familiar—I urge you to read on, with an open mind, and consider the possibility that you may be an unidentified gifted adult.

More often than not, I come across very smart people who have no idea that some of the aspects of their personality are actually peculiarities of being gifted. Sometimes, they consider these to be character flaws; other times, they're just "quirks." Upon learning about giftedness, they frequently are relieved of a lifetime of confusion and misunderstanding (and other times it makes them angry—really really angry). It takes a good deal of introspection and hard work to look inside yourself and really dig into the stories you've always told yourself. It can be pretty scary. Defining your own sense of your giftedness is a personal journey and personal struggle.

What does this have to do with intensity? Well, gifted people tend to be very intense, in pretty much everything they do. They have a wide variety of interests, and want to master them all. They are intensely curious and want to know ALL of the "whys." They dig for answers—probably more than most people care for. Intense people can easily offend, distance, and put off others by simply being themselves.

There are as many definitions of giftedness as there are people in the world—every one of us is a snowflake (in the best sense of the word) and we each have our own way of defining what makes us gifted. It's not all about being book-smart or academically high-achieving, and you don't have to be a musical prodigy. Instead, you might be empathically gifted or gifted in sports; you may be a scientist, or a business leader who has done very well in his or her field. The varieties are endless.

Many gifted adults are unaware of how giftedness affects their lives. Some seem to do fine and the characteristics of giftedness do not pose a problem in their everyday lives; others could use insight into the whole topic, because they feel helpless to conquer these challenges. My clients often tell me that they're told they're too intense, and friends and family don't know how to deal with their intensity, so it's no wonder that they don't know what to do with it. It can feel like you're broken or you just don't fit in anywhere.

On the other hand, you may already know that you're gifted—but you just can't figure out how to make it work for you. Although awareness is the first step, it's not the only step. This book is for entrepreneurs who want to make their business do more with less work, whether you're gifted or not. Gifted people are typically entrepreneurial by nature but may not know how to put it all together in one place and make it go in the right direction.

This book provides practical advice for handling the challenges that gifted individuals have; you'll be able to recognize, honor, and use your quirks as your business superpowers. It is not another formula, or more generic business advice from the internet. You don't need to use someone else's process —you need to find your own. This book is your guide to finding your unique process and unique voice, so that you can do your business your way. You'll learn how to lead yourself and stop following everyone else.

Being an entrepreneur is usually a rocky road. There are ups and downs that are uncontrollable and unpredictable — it doesn't always go like you'd planned. When you're this intense, that is how life is. Intensity in giftedness means you are more emotional, go deeper with your investigation and intuition, and see things in greater detail than most people around you. That can work for you and make you very profitable, or against you, if you let it get out of control. When intensities get out of control, you may never recover.

I wrote this book because I see so many entrepreneurs who don't understand how to get their message out in a way that reaches their best audience. They struggle and then feel worse, like no one will ever understand them and no one will be able to benefit from what they have to offer. My clients are intense people who do have great gifts to share with the world, but just can't seem to get them in front of the right audience. They are strong, compassionate, smart, and driven. There is no reason they shouldn't be living the lifestyles they dream of.

Now is the time for you to change perspectives, reframe your life as you know it, and get into the driver's seat. Now you can take control of those intensities and turn them into your best assets. They don't have to be your downfall.

Like many coaches, I came to this industry as a part of my own self-discovery and healing. It's taken me over 40 years to come to the happy place I'm at now, and I love being able to help others find that place for themselves.

It wasn't easy, though.

I spent a long time thinking I was not very bright, troubled in some way or another, and generally irresponsible. I felt unlikeable, unlovable, and like I didn't fit in.

I stumbled upon my own giftedness as the result of having my kids tested. The pains I've felt most of my life have actually been related to the challenges of being gifted. When most people hear "the G-word," they think, "smart." But when I hear it, I think, "underachiever, perfectionist, impostor syndrome, unrealistically idealistic, too intense, scattered, overly sensitive/emotional, unmotivated, too many interests," and some other not-very-nice stories I've told myself over the years.

I took six years to get my undergraduate degree, and I ended up designing it myself because nothing already created suited me. I sailed through most of my undergraduate classes, not realizing that I actually had no idea how to study; I just sat in class and regurgitated that information on the test. I thought that was normal (see *procrastination* in Chapter 1).

When I was accepted to medical school, I thought it was a fluke. I went anyway, just holding my breath and waiting for them to discover that I didn't deserve to be there. And guess what? Medical school is hard—for everyone, even the smartest students. The volume of new information was something I'd never encountered and it quickly overwhelmed me—I figured that even if they never realized I didn't belong,

I would surely flunk out (see *impostor syndrome* in Chapter 1).

In my first semester of medical school, 9-11 happened. And a month later my father died, secondary to his massive heart attack a year earlier. And a month after that my aunt was killed in a car accident. But I kept on going and pushed through (because that's how I cope), and within a couple years I met a great man and had wonderful babies. We soon decided it would be best for me to stay home with them, so I sacrificed my medical career for my family (see Chapter 1 for a description of *fear of success*).

While at home, I quickly became bored and thought I was a broken mother, incapable of giving the kids what they needed because I didn't want to stay at home all day and coo at them. Although I loved them dearly, that just wasn't enough for me (more of the *intellectual over-excitability*). So I got my master's degree in nonprofit management, filed for divorce, and started a whole new life with my kids.

Shortly after the divorce, my children's father died, which forced me back into the workforce and I had to figure out what I would do with my life that would meet all of my needs and also support my family. After spending a year doing hospital work, I finally realized that entrepreneurship was where I belonged, and specifically in coaching because it allows me to help people while also getting my own needs fulfilled. The most important part of entrepreneurship, for me, is that I am able to be fully present for my kids.

As it turns out, the things I need are the things most gifted people need from their work: autonomy, creativity, problem-solving, and helping people. I am able to help those with challenges that are not only hidden, but stigmatized—that is priceless to me. Giftedness is not nearly as much a blessing as a curse, and my hope some day is to help everyone understand what it really means to be gifted, to accept the struggles that are invisible.

There are all kinds of tests and assessments you can do to find out what you're like as a person, including those that measure giftedness. Although they all have value, and I use them every day in my work, those tests will only tell you so much about how you answered the questions. At our core, because of the way we were raised, we all have stories that we've learned about ourselves and we tell ourselves those stories over and over.

When I became an entrepreneur, I changed my story from feeling like a failure at life to being in total control of my world. It took a lot of introspection and the help of a number of people that supported me during my challenges. I took up the pen, became my own author, and re-wrote what my future looked like.

You are the author of your story, and as such, you can change the course of the story, the plot, and the depth—and you alone can create a character that you love. I am grateful that you've given me the opportunity to help guide you through this awesome transition.

With all of that said, I'll point out that knowledge isn't a shortcut to critical thinking, and knowing is just a springboard for doing. I'm walking beside you to get to the watering hole. You're still walking on your own (I'm not carrying you), and you're still going to need to find your own cup to drink from (and then drink!). You will need to think through each activity and ponder how it relates to you and your business, and then apply it in your own way, to what you do. Consider me inspiration for your own metacognitive process that will lead you to action.

How to Use This Book

This book can serve as a reference, a guide or roadmap, or a means of checks and balances for your intensity. Because your brain accelerates towards a goal based on the progress it thinks it's already made, you should keep track of your work and celebrate all the small goals. This is one way to practice breaking goals into smaller, more digestible parts, but it also serves as a way to celebrate your success. Don't forget daily reminders of gratitude and self-compassion. You probably should create an achievement board or file folder (whatever makes the most sense to you), to look at daily, to remind yourself that you've come a long way and you've got what it takes.

In a year or even six months, come back to this book and re-work the activities, re-think your thoughts again. How have things changed? Have you achieved what you wanted to? Have your goals changed?

In this book you will find:

- discussion about your intensity, and why you may be "too much" for some people
- stories that are amalgamations of my

clients and close friends, used to illustrate particular points

- direction on how to find your most authentic voice
- tips and ideas on how to be successful with your quirks.

Chapter 1 talks about intensity and giftedness. You will have an opportunity to explore the concepts of giftedness, to be free with your curiosity about whether you may be gifted, and to understand what it's like to be gifted. If nothing else, this chapter serves as education about how difficult it can be to feel this world so intensely.

In *Chapter 2* we will find your most authentic voice. Being in business for yourself is a scary, rocky road, with unique challenges. This chapter will help you find your unique voice so that it's not so scary and you can reach the audience that's full of your ideal clients or customers.

Chapter 3 is all about leadership within

the context of entrepreneurship. Just starting a business does not guarantee that you will make money; you will need to dedicate time, money, and energy to being a leader in your one-woman organization.

In *Chapter 4* we will talk about networking for the intense entrepreneur. When you are an introvert, networking can be a not-so-subtle form of torture. Although there are plenty of extroverts, many gifted people are introverts, making it tough to network and get out to self-promote. Here, you will find a way to feel good about reaching out.

Chapter 5 is about sales and marketing. This is another tricky area, because you may feel that, with a great product or service, it should sell itself. Not so. Everyone, at every level, has to sell their stuff; this chapter will help you find how to do it in a way that feels less like sales and more like sharing something awesome.

In *Chapter 6* we will discuss community and collaboration. Your community will be a integral part of your networking, sales, marketing, and the general success of your business. Collaboration is a way to expand that community to grow your reach and your impact, if you choose to go that route.

Chapter 7 is for scaling and sustainability. Scaling is how you can, if you want to, scale your business up and make it bigger—but keep track of retaining sustainable practices for you to continue using for the foreseeable future.

In *Chapter 8* we will tie it all together and look at the big picture; step back and look at your business with a wide lens, while detaching (just for a moment) from the details.

Appendix A is a list of references where you will find all the resources I used for writing this book.

Appendix B is full of all the questions and prompts you'll need to do the work in this book. Flip through this appendix before you start in Chapter 1 so that you're ready to work.

Appendix C has the lists referenced in Chapters 2 and 4-6.

Although you can read each chapter separately and, to a degree, compartmentalize the information contained within them, the ideas here are not independent of each other. You can't talk about sales without talking about leadership, because you can't sell your products unless someone trusts you and they can't trust you if you're not being an effective leader. It all ties together. It's a system, just like everything in life.

Let's get to work, shall we?

1
What is Intensity?

You might have purchased this book thinking, "I'm intense, but I'm not gifted" or "I'm no good at academics, so I can't be gifted"—but you're curious. Well, let me ask you some questions.

Have these words been used to describe you: overly excitable, unmanageable, impossible, unsatisfied, insatiable, hyperactive, unadaptable, obstinate, or undisciplined? Have you been told that you come on too strong, you're a spaz, you've got too much energy, you have too much imagination (not realistic), and/or you're too flighty? What other words have you heard to describe your intense personality?

Although they may seem like separate ideas, intensity and giftedness are not independent of each other. Giftedness is something that everyone defines differently, and in fact, many highly intelligent people are not successful in an academic setting. Just Google "world schooling" or "unschooling" as well as homeschooling, to see evidence of the alternative lifestyles of highly gifted people who do not fit in in a classroom.

One of my save-the-world ideas is to have the word "gifted" be more widely accepted among the general population. At this time, it is not, and the G-word is more likely associated with arrogance. I want it to be okay for anyone to talk about giftedness, but I realize we're not there yet. For now, right here, it's okay to talk about giftedness, just like it's okay to talk about being an introvert, having breast cancer, or being gay. And—it's okay to say that you don't think you're gifted, as well. The chances are good that if you're wondering, and if you're reading this book, you probably are, in some form of the definition. But whatever your personal experience, there is total acceptance here.

This introduction to giftedness and intensity is just the tip of the iceberg, the part above the surface—you'll have to find the bottom of it by going under the surface, by being really honest with yourself and digging into what you do and don't know about yourself. Because of the intense introspection required, this part of the self-discovery process can be a bit (or a lot) scary. I know; I've been there.

At this point it should be noted that not everyone has challenges with giftedness. Some people are gifted, and don't know it, and it makes absolutely no difference when they discover it. One of my friends is a man who works independently in international development. He knows multiple languages, travels overseas many times per year helping organizations in small countries to work through their various problems, and help their communities and citizens. When I told him he was gifted, he sort of shrugged it off. In getting to know him, I realized that he doesn't have any problems with giftedness. He copes well with everything he does. These characteristics never get out of control for him—and he's an awesome, fun, interesting guy. He was surprised to know that it's not "normal" that his 2 year-old is already reading, so it seems that gifted parenting may be his first challenge in the realm of giftedness.

This man's reaction is not the most common response I experience when people learn about their own giftedness. It is typically quite different, which is why this and many other books are written about the experience of being gifted. Although there is currently way more support for children, the gifted adult community is growing. The reason for that is likely related to so many parents having their kids tested and learning about their own giftedness in the process of learning how to support and advocate for their children.

Sadly, the generally accepted perspective on giftedness goes straight to something along the lines of exceptionality in academics and/or intelligence. Although many gifted people can be advanced or high achieving in academic pursuits, not everyone is gifted in that way. Some may be intellectually gifted, while others may be emotionally gifted or artistically gifted. Heck, some gifted people don't even *like* math!

Perhaps a better definition of giftedness needs to come from intensity.

Intensity could be defined as exceptional force or energy (Merriam-Webster), as applied to, and in the context of, everything we do. That could mean that you come on "too strong" when you're really excited or anxious about something, which can pose a problem when you're trying to promote yourself. Alternatively, it could mean that you get stuck on subjects and can't move on.

Regardless of the flavor of intensity, there are definite consistencies in the way gifted people exist: we are intensely curious, need depth in our interaction, and conceptualize ideas faster than most people. Gifted individuals are not just good at their area of expertise—they're intensely immersed in the experience of learning to master it, intensely invested in knowing their vocation to the same extent that they feel it, and enthusiastically excited to share it with everyone in the whole wide world.

Below you will find some very general and superficial descriptions of many characteristics of giftedness. It is not exhaustive and not in the depth you may be seeking. There is an extensive list of recommended reading for more information on giftedness and the experience of being gifted. As you work through this chapter, you may recognize some characteristics in yourself.

Here we go!

There are a constellation of characteristics of giftedness, some of which I will not discuss, but below is a short list of *some* of them with some descriptions following that. Sidebar to note that, taken alone, each of these could be their own issues; rather, it is the combination of many of these characteristics that paint a picture of giftedness or intensity (it's sort of an I-know-it-when-I-see-it type of thing).

- Multi-potentiality
- Perfectionism
- Procrastination
- Fear of failure
- Fear of success
- Existential depression
- Anxiety
- Gifts and challenges of being an outlier
- Introversion/extroversion

- Spiritual sensitivity and heartfelt intuition
- Amplified ways of being
- Sensitivity and intensity
- Misdiagnosis and dual diagnosis (twice exceptional)
- Interpersonal challenges
- Career challenges
- Finding personal meaning
- Creativity

Depth/Curiosity/Intensity/Complexity

What drives gifted people can best be expressed as an unquenchable thirst for depth, an unspoken knowledge that things are always more complex than they initially look, and a seeking of intensity (in work, relationships, experience, you name it).

Gifted people have a huge range of interests and can be all over the place with the subjects they want to study—but always to great depth. For example, one of my clients plays the violin, studies psychology, teaches pottery, and is also a stay-at-home mom of twins. Their family is really big into cycling, so they are intensely into mountain biking (her husband teaches it and supports their family with it). She also lifts weights in an academic way—meaning she's scientifically accurate about her workouts. With multiple undergraduate degrees, she is no slouch in academics, but feels like she doesn't know anything or hasn't achieved much in her life.

This leads into the next cluster of characteristics of giftedness, some of which have been publicized a lot lately on social media: perfectionism, procrastination, introversion, and impostor syndrome. These characteristics often (but not always) run together and can cause havoc in your life, even leading, in the most severe case, to agoraphobia. When left unchecked, these qualities can be devastating to anyone, and can destroy a business that took years to establish.

Perfectionism

Perfectionism seems nice on the surface. Who wouldn't want to do a great job all the time and be driven to make the best products and be the best at everything? When it gets out of control, you will have an intimate understanding of why you don't want it to get out of control. You can't get anything done! If everything has to be perfect, then nothing ever is. Perfectionism has roots in childhood, when approval was super important to you and achievement became a top priority. Giving children praise for achievement is, in the long run, not healthy because they end up only wanting (needing) that praise for end results. Ergo, perfectionism.

Perfectionism can also be a problem when an individual creates unrealistic expectations for themselves. When you have to be 100% all the time, you're bound to feel like a failure when you don't achieve, get sick, or otherwise aren't feeling up to snuff (and them impostor syndrome lies on some stress (see below)).

Introvertedness(is that a word? spellcheck says no. I say yes.)

Introversion is not, per se, a problem. To me, an introvert, it's no big deal. Except that I know that if I let it get out of control, I will never leave the house. It is a constant struggle to balance the need to get out (and see people and converse) with the need to be alone (and process the day, in order to take care of myself). Extroverts don't usually get it, and that's okay. Please read up on anything that Susan Cain writes, as she is a fantastic speaker and author that talks about the ways that being an introvert can be very powerful.

Impostor Syndrome

Impostor syndrome can be debilitating and knows no boundaries. It can strike even the most famous and talented people: Jodie Foster, Denzel Washington, and Maya Angelou, just to name a few. All incredible, right? All have said something along the lines of "They're going to find out that I'm a fraud". Not only does it behave retroactively (they'll figure out I'm a fraud and don't deserve to be here), it also works to prevent you from starting new projects (I can't do that because I don't know enough about it). After all, if you feel like you don't deserve the accolades you've received in the past, why would you venture out and hatch new ideas?

Fear of success plays a part in impostor syndrome because you may not feel that you're qualified to take on the additional responsibility of succeeding in your endeavors. For example, when I was in medical school, I did great in my didactics and clinicals, and when it came time to graduate, I was terrified. The thought of being truly responsible for people's lives the day after graduation was ridiculous to me.

Easily Distracted in a Deep Way (aka Feeling Scattered) (aka Shiny Object Syndrome)

This can be a real problem for anyone, but particularly for the intense person. Because you need to master the things you devote precious time to, you can really get sucked into a vortex with each new thing that comes along promising untold gold and riches. Okay, that's a little overly dramatic, but I know you know what I'm talking about. When you get distracted, it can draw you away from the real work you *need* to do. Keeping this in check is not easy, but when you have a focus for your business, it will become a bit easier.

Procrastination is also at play here, because gifted individuals can often seemingly pull great and wonderful things out of thin air but they actually waited until the last minute. This was evident in my own school experience, because I was rewarded with top grades when I waited until the last minute to get my work done (and then underachievement kicked in and stopped me from wanting to get a better grade by doing more work). Interestingly, I saw how wrong it was, but couldn't find a way to stop it.

Empaths and Sensitivity

Taking Dąbrowski's emotional OE just one step further is where we find empaths. Empaths are people who not only feel their own emotions and energy deeply (like being a highly sensitive person), but they also feel it from the people around them. It's like being plugged into other people and not being able to disconnect. You can imagine how chaotic that can be when you don't know what it is. Some people describe this as colors or images, or a general feeling or sensation, while others describe it as energy or light.

People who are empathic can tend to take on problems that are not theirs to take. This extreme emotional sensitivity can also lead to existential depression—the sense that this universe is so big and so broken that there's no point in trying to change it. Or, in another form, we are so small that there's no way we can have the impact we want to. In yet another form, existential depression is expressed by children trying to find meaning in life and the world, and finding it a little bit ... lacking. It should be no surprise that there are a lot of suicides among gifted individuals.

Multi-Potentiality

As mentioned previously, gifted people typically don't have just one thing they like to do. A good variety of names have been invented to address this, with the most accurate (in my opinion) being multi-potentialite, but you may also have heard such a person referred to as a scanner, polymath, expert-generalist, Renaissance person, etc. This type of person may have one job for a long time, but it has to be something that allows huge amounts of autonomy, flexibility, and creativity. It's more common that the multi-potentialite switches jobs frequently, or takes jobs (or creates them through entrepreneurship) that allow all of their interests to be explored concurrently. Music, art, creative expression, science, culture, business, and growth may all be deep interests of one multi-potentialite.

The way each gifted person dives into their areas of interest can vary; for example, some like to go all in for each subject, spending a lot of time and energy on that one idea, then dropping it completely for the next idea. Or maybe they dabble in each area, but have 20 things going on all at the same time. Yet another way this can be expressed is when a person goes through phases of interest, such as seasonal interaction with hobbies.

Multi-potentiality doesn't look as obviously destructive as most other characteristics of giftedness when it's out of control. It looks like you're scattered, flaky, and maybe can't hold down a decent job. Usually this isn't stopping you from progressing, but it has great potential to do so.

Big (Huge) Ideas and Metacognition

One of the major themes I've noticed with gifted people is that they have huge ideas about saving the world. We have a strong sense of justice and want to help others, leading to a more developed ability for metacognition than most people. We often think deeply about thinking and why we do what we do and how that plays out.

Generally speaking, metacognition is more developed in those with more experience, both in life and in metacognition (yes, thinking about thinking begets more/better/faster thinking about thinking). They have seen more situations, experienced more alternative solutions, and know the value of trying things out before committing to one course of action. Visualizing alternative solutions is easier with more varied experiences, and thus makes metacognition more feasible.

In comparison, people new to the experience, and less adept with metacognition, would more often take a known path or solution, be less likely to try new things, and would eventually learn that this is not an effective way to get things done.

Let's take surgeons as an example. New surgeons haven't seen much, although they have a good basic foundation of knowledge. What makes surgeons great is their experience and what they've learned from those experiences. They are able to think through the possible solutions and outcomes. This is how metacognition works—the more experience you have, the greater the depth you can reach with thinking about thinking. Because gifted thinkers get overall concepts faster, they get the experiences of thinking faster than a non-gifted person.

Strategic methods that focus on metacognition for deeper learning have been shown to result in more permanent learning gains, including developing a growth mindset, setting and monitoring one's learning goals, and growing one's capacity to persist despite difficulties.

Metacognition is on a positive reinforcement loop, meaning that those who use it successfully will continue to use it, increasing effectiveness as they become more experienced. Those who do not use it will become less effective or stay the same, not improving because they have no signs of success.

Metacognition gets in the way when you allow it to consume your day (unless that's what you get paid to do, in which case, bravo!). You can't live your life thinking about thinking all day. Hopefully, developing skills in metacognition allows you to have greater impact in what you do get paid to do!

Dąbrowski's Overexcitabilities

Overexcitabilities (OEs) are something that you never hear of unless you are studying psychology or a parent that is trying to understand how to support their gifted child(ren). The OEs Dąbrowski described were his way of defining flavors of intensity in kids; I see them as intense coping mechanisms. They are:

- *Sensual*—liking (needing) soft clothes and self-soothing sensations, hating seams and tags in clothes
- *Emotional*—deeply, intensely emotional, possibly to the point of being an empath
- *Intellectual*—needing a constant flow of new information; always asking why/how
- *Imaginational*—always living in the imagination, regardless of age (think Walt Disney); difficulty distinguishing between real and imaginary
- *Psychomotor*—a need to move in order to hear or learn (commonly misdiagnosed as ADD/ADHD)

Dąbrowski's Theory of Positive Disintegration

The Theory of Positive Disintegration (TPD) is a huge topic, and I can't possibly address it all here. I'll talk a little bit more about it in the next chapter, but basically says that when we're feeling like we're unraveling and don't know what to do (get stuck), it's actually an incredible jumping-off point that is a new beginning for learning and growth. There's way more to it, but that's a very surface description version.

School Experience of the Gifted Person

As you can probably imagine, descriptions of school experiences are all over the place, because everyone is different in their learning, background, and the way they were raised, not to mention that many people don't understand their own (highly individual) learning process. Just being identified as gifted in younger years does not guarantee a healthy and happy school experience. Neither does *not* being identified. With that said, it seems that happy and healthy parents have a lot to do with your school experience because your parents can make or break your outlook on life.

My own experience, as someone who was never identified in school as gifted and had divorced parents, was fraught with misunderstandings about who I was and what I was meant to do on this Earth. I thought I was doing okay (just average) until I got to medical school. That's when I learned, the hard way, that I had no clue how to study. And I didn't even know *why* I didn't know how. My conclusion was that I must have been ridiculously dense. I didn't know about overwhelm (too much volume of information, a lack of understanding of how I learn best), or test taking strategy, or actual study strategies. Executive function skills (organizational skills) were not my friends at that point in my life.

I think that the best way to make school a good experience is to know yourself very well, know how to keep yourself happy in terms of OEs and sensitivity needs (various types of stimuli), having study skills, and knowing your personal learning style. Of course, there is no shortage of opinions on how to make school work the best for each student. There are entire communities built on Facebook for just this purpose. Regardless of how you find the support, each student should know how they learn and what they need (no matter what age they are), which is mostly a matter of introspection.

The overall school experience of an intense/gifted person can be good or bad, high-achieving or low-achieving. Having multiple degrees does not mean it was easy, nor does it mean that the student can't "settle" on a subject. Being a multi-potentialite can cause a great amount of strife in a person's life if they are expressing that in the school setting, bouncing from one degree or major to the next.

Additionally, college may not be the right solution for some gifted people. Some kids are entrepreneurs before reaching high school, and some are founders of nonprofit organizations. If college isn't right, or too restrictive, or not supportive enough, then for the sake of all that is holy, *don't make your kids go!* These days, college is a risky endeavor. There are too many kids who go to college and end up no better in the end; some don't make it through at all (and the financial cost of that should not be underestimated). Take your child's unique situation into consideration before you try to make them get a degree they don't want and won't use, at a school that may be a dangerous place for their sensitive personalities.

You may very well be out of school and feel that you're done with it, so why bother talking about it? Well, because I've found that many gifted adults are a bit ... addicted ... to education and school. It may be the intellectual OE, or just the deep curiosity of the gifted mind—either way, we *love* to learn! And it doesn't stop when you get out of high school or when you finish an undergraduate degree (or your second or third graduate degrees).

Work Experience of the Gifted Person

Gifted people work in every area, every industry, and are even creating new fields and new technologies because the traditional framework doesn't allow them to function at optimal levels. At the very least, the work environment of a gifted person needs to provide autonomy, opportunity for creativity, and be intellectually stimulating and engaging. Without those characteristics, the gifted employee with become disengaged and eventually will leave, get fired, or both.

Testing for Adults

The reasons behind testing are personal, for each individual, and it's up to you whether or not to get tested. The full battery of tests is expensive and many adults don't have the resources to take a $2,000 test. Sadly, there isn't really another inexpensive option for adults other than the Mensa entrance exam (which is pass/fail, and does not provide you with a number score). Not taking a test or having an IQ number does not mean that you are not gifted. It just means you haven't had it quantified. There is a quiz you can take, in the book *The Gifted Adult* by Mary-Elaine Jacobsen, that is fairly inexpensive (the price of the book is around $13) and it seems to be a reasonable estimation of IQ. It should only be used as a screening tool, though, not as a final report. You can really only get that from a full test by a certified psychologist

Testing for Kids

Although not within the scope of this book, I think it's important to note how kids are tested, simply because so many of my clients are parents of gifted kids, and that's frequently how they stumble on their own giftedness. Kids are tested in a formal setting, usually by a psychologist or neuropsychologist. It's a whole thing—much more formal and documented so that you can advocate for your child in their school system. You can look in the resource appendix for more info on that.

TIME TO ACT

Now it's time to do some work. This chapter and the next one will be very labor-intensive, but it will get a little bit easier after that.

1. Intensities

First, list out your challenges that you have in your business. Use the list of characteristics I created above, or use Paula Prober's book (*Your Rainforest Mind*) or any other books on intensity and/or giftedness. Or just write out your challenges as you see them. You don't have to label them as "gifted" if you're not comfortable with that. These challenges are your intensities.

Now consider your intensities in the context of your business. Can you get an idea of how you can flip your intensities to your advantage with these activities, by using moderation to keep them in check? How can you reframe them so that you can use them to your advantage?

Here are some examples of flipping intensities.

Strength	Intensity	Quirk
Produce great services and products	Perfectionism	Can't move on, can't finish
Evaluate all options and see various outcomes	Procrastination	Wait until last minute to complete tasks
Get really deep into subjects when most people only see surface value	Depth	Get tunnel vision and be unable to finish multiple tasks
Asking questions no one else thinks of	Curiosity	Shiny object syndrome, easily distracted
Wide array of skills and educational background	Multi-potentiality	Scattered, jump from job to job

2. Overall Goal

Next, we'll work on your overall goal for your business, for the short long term (six to twelve months). There are a plethora of terms you could use for the overall goal, but I like "Chief Initiative." Coined by

Tara Gentile, this term implies action, leadership, and energy—it says that this is a big goal, it's an umbrella (overall coverage for your business), and yet it's not an endpoint but a beginning. It's where you want to be in six to twelve months, and it reflects what you dream of for your business—big, wild, wonderful dreams, the kind you don't want to wake up from.

Put that Chief Initiative into the context of your specific intensities. Do you face perfectionism or any other challenges I listed? How will you address that, with your Chief Initiative? What about impostor syndrome? How are you going to conquer that, and still accomplish your Chief Initiative?

Your Chief Initiative needs to be *SMART:*

- Specific
- Measurable
- Achievable

- Realistic
- Time-bound

For example, you can't just say, "I want to have a successful business in twelve months." That's too vague, because who knows what the definition of success is, and it could change in twelve months. It's not measurable or achievable. A realistic goal would be, "I will have ten full-time clients per month, and offer six courses during the year." Or maybe it could be, "I will have produced 1,000 of my specialty items and 5,000 of the lower model, in 6 months or less." Whatever your business, you need to have a goal that follows the SMART rules.

3. Sub-Goals

Now you'll need to create sub-goals, which are the things you need to do to make the Chief Initiative happen. Everything you do, in the next six to twelve months, will be in pursuit of the Chief Initiative, so what will those steps need to be? Is your C.I. to write a book? What research do you need to do first, what software do you need to buy or learn, and what editor/publisher will you use? Is your C.I. to have 20 clients by the end of the year? What will you need to do on social media or other marketing outlets to find those clients? What emails will you need to send? What offerings will you provide to promote your brand?

More Information

This is really just a small sampling of the challenges of intensity and giftedness and how they can help or hinder you and your work. I have found that this journey is personal and self-paced—you need to get the information you need, when you need it and when you are able to fully receive it. To that end, Appendix A is an extensive list of resources recommended for your journey of discovering what it means to be gifted.

2
Finding Your Voice

As an entrepreneur, you have many choices that you wouldn't otherwise have. Some are fun, like designing your brand, and some aren't, like figuring out how to get your message across succinctly. As an intense person, you may tend to be verbose, or possibly the opposite (overly concise). All the stuff has to get done, both fun and not-so-fun, and it's hard to do that when fear, doubt, and other challenges creep up on you to stop you from getting your message out.

The story you tell with your message, the products or services you sell, the audience you speak to—this is the expression of your voice. It should communicate who you are. The decisions you make in expressing your voice can really put the kibosh on whether visitors convert (no pressure, right?). If you're choosing not to use your "real" voice, you may not attract the your ideal clients.

Likewise, your audience has a choice, and their decisions are based on whether they like what you say (i.e., how you make them feel). If they like it, they'll consume it and share it.

Fear and Doubt

As entrepreneurs, we have great ideas running around in our heads, but fear gets in and says the risk is too great; doubts creep by and whisper that you're not qualified; "what ifs" trample you to death with possible negative outcomes. It can hold you back entirely from even starting a business, but you've got to work through the fears, doubts, and "what ifs" in order to get to your authentic voice.

Gifted individuals fuel that fire with intense imaginations, impostor syndrome, and perfectionism (among other things). Yes, we can see the great world that *could be* if we only had unlimited time and funds; we can also see our whole lives being destroyed by making one stupid move. We over-analyze like no others, and create negative self-talk stories that hold us hostage from ever getting a proper start.

But people do survive and get through. You did, or you wouldn't be reading this book; or maybe you're looking for the extra push to go ahead. Everyone needs some extra encouragement at times.

In order to get to know yourself and your voice, you have to spend time with—and make space for—failure and success. Losses and gains both have something to teach. The data you collect, when you analyze it like a scientist, will become the foundation of your good choices in the future. The more data you have, the higher the chances of making great choices next time. If you think of the data points as snowflakes, you can see that independently they are fairly insignificant, but collectively they can be more substantive.

On one hand, finding your voice is easy, because it's just about knowing yourself. On the other hand, it can be tough, because you may not know *how to express that.* I've found that the best way to get it your true voice is to: do some soul-searching (with the help of the work at the end of this chapter), and then start writing. Write in a journal or a blog, or whatever medium you prefer, but make sure that you're writing to your target audience. When you have that ideal client in your head as the reader, you will be much more in tune with what they would like to read, thus making your writing more resonant with them. In the know-like-trust progression, resonance is how you get the reader from "know" to "like." They read what you write, and they like it; your message and values resonate with them, and they relate to it. If you have written in your most authentic voice, with your ideal client in mind, the ones who are not ideal will move on, allowing you the time and energy to focus on the ones you do click with.

As you write, you're going to build up a collection—a body of work—that will begin to show your flavor, your brand, and your personality. That's your voice and your personality, which will develop over time. Your voice is the battle-ax that fights fear and doubt; knowing yourself and what you stand for is the best way to quiet fear and push doubt down. For now, let's start with a beginning definition of what your authentic voice sounds like.

The way I see it, your voice starts with your core values, which are expressed through your preferences. To find your preferences and the language of those preferences, you will do a couple of assessments that I have all my clients do: the Myers-Briggs personality test and the Fascination Advantage assessment. But before we can even get to those steps, we have to backtrack and talk about some of the things no one likes to talk about—fear, doubt, and negative self-talk.

For the gifted and intense individual, fears, doubts, and negative self-talk and stories we tell ourselves are amplified—to eleven. We establish a death grip that is astonishingly difficult to loosen. The really great thing is that, when you're that good at the negative stuff, you know you've got the same potential for the positive stuff. Your voice is the expression of that. When you find it, you get to be yourself and the people who are drawn to that are your people.

I can't tell you how many times I've heard, "I'm too intense," from clients and other gifted individuals who are just too much for other people. My response is that those aren't *your* people. Your community is full of people who get your intensity and hear your message, and they like both.

The same things that can prevent you from starting can also hold you down after you've made success and gotten some traction. You need some coping skills for dealing with them. If I learned anything from my kids' therapist, it's that you can't back away from fear, you can't deny it, and you can't stuff it away. A lot of "gurus" will tell you to be fearless—but that's not how emotional intelligence works. If you don't acknowledge the fear and doubt, you'll remain stuck.

You have to name it to tame it, sit with it a bit, and then bid it adieu. I know, easier said than done, right? And yet, totally doable with practice.

There's an animated Irish movie my kids love, called *Song of the Sea*. It's about a young boy and his sister, who lose their mother when the girl is born (he blames his sister for the loss of his mother, and is kind of horrible to her for quite some time).

They go on an epic journey together, and all the while, something magical is happening inside the girl. She's a selkie, which means she's supposed to sing in order to free fairies, but she hasn't uttered a sound since her mother died; not singing is slowly killing her. One of the villains in the movie is an old woman (in owl form) who traps people's bad emotions in jars (sadness, anger, loneliness, etc.). She caps them off and keeps them in her attic, and with every negative emotion of her own that she traps, her body progressively turns to stone. When the girl finally sings, it shatters the jars, frees the emotions and the fairies, and turns everyone whole again.

The symbolism should be fairly obvious here, but if it's not, it means that bottling up your painful emotions is just not good for you. I love this movie because it teaches my kids emotional intelligence, but it's also a good reminder for me to take care of myself and my own emotions.

When we can recognize and acknowledge fear, and go forward anyway, it does something special for each of us, as well as the world outside our heads. You can practice self-compassion with yourself, for being human, which in turn allows you to be more compassionate with everyone else. You respect yourself by acknowledging that you're human, which allows you to see the human side of everyone else. And the double bonus is that once you've faced your fears, you're going to be more confident that they can't touch you. You become more and more resilient and the fears and doubt become smaller and smaller. And just like metacognition, the more experience we gain in this skill, the better we become at it.

Assumptions and Negative Self-Talk

Although much of life is out of your control, there are a great number of things you can control. It's definitely a learning process and you have to train yourself to think in terms of *probabilities* as well as *pos-*

sibilities. With training, you'll be able to imagine a variety of scenarios, a spectrum of outcomes, and in time you can develop your intuition about where the good stuff is and where it is not. You can train yourself to stop thinking in assumptions.

This is called "Bayesian" thinking or instinct, and basically it says that when we make assumptions and forget to consider other perspectives, we miss considering very different outcomes. By assuming, we limit our thinking, our beliefs, and our outcomes.

Switching out of assumptions is easier said than done, because we rely heavily on our past experiences and all the jacked-up psychology (aka baggage) that goes with them. And we often have a whole belief system to back up the baggage on all the reasons we're making mistakes.

We like believing the BS! We back it up, support it, and justify it, which is, in and of itself, BS.

Moving out of assumptions and into a

Bayesian mindset requires experimentation and flexible thinking (and visualization doesn't hurt). Tweak something in your business, gather data, interpret the results, adjust, and update incrementally. Knowing the effect of your adjustments in your business will give you access to incredible new answers you can't get to with assumptions. Of course, you can't just go willy-nilly, changing everything at the same time, because then you never know what the cause was. Change one thing at a time, track it, reflect on the results. What comes out of your experiment and, more importantly, what can you learn from it?

In addition to tweaking your business experimentally, you can utilize visualization to practice Bayesian thinking. By seeing alternative outcomes in your mind, you open yourself to all the possibilities and stop making assumptions. You give yourself the freedom to see what's beyond the assumptions.

Reframing

There are so many ways to deal with fear and doubt; one technique, utilized by both coaches and therapists, is reframing. It's probably the most effective technique I've found for finding a new perspective. When we make assumptions, it limits our thinking; reframing allows us to evaluate alternative ways of thinking and solving problems. Reframing is accomplished pretty simply: just imagine yourself in someone else's shoes. Think about who they are, what their background may be, and why they make the decisions they make. I do this in a variety of settings. For example, I imagine myself as my clients, so that I can try to give them the best coaching experience possible. I imagine myself as my kids, so that I can try to give them the best parenting possible.

Reframing is a method for finding perspective, but it's also a solid modality for locking in empathy and compassion. Sidebar to note that there is a great table at the end of this chapter to see how you can moderate the quirks to be strengths by using reframing.

Another reframing trick is to ask yourself a different kind of "what if." For example, when you're feeling like your emails aren't getting through to your clients, you can ask, "what if I didn't send any emails?" Or "what if I sent more emails?" Or "what if my emails aren't worded as effectively as they could be?"

When we do the negative self-talk and reinforce our negative stories, it's done out of fear, but also out of love. You don't want yourself to feel the pain that lies beneath the negative stories. Of course, it's a bad cycle that doesn't really help you in the long run, but that's how we work. We save ourselves from the pain now, because it's immediate. And the deeper you bury it, the more it grows, just like in the movie *Song of the Sea*.

Ask yourself the following four questions and you'll be on your way to healthy self-compassion and reframing your thinking.

1. Is this concept/idea/thought true?

If you can have a realistic perspective, you can stop the negative self-talk right here. That can be hard when impostor syndrome has gotten out of control. Think about what someone else would say about your thought. Would they agree or disagree?

2. What evidence do I have?

We do love to support and back up all of our negative talk, because not doing so would shatter our reality. Most people don't want their reality shattered, because it's what makes them feel safe. This step requires you to really come up with hard, tangible evidence. Take a close look at whether you're trying to support your thoughts with judgments (I'm a failure) or facts (I'm not getting straight A's). You want to make sure you're not using the former as a basis for self-esteem. Try to stick only to facts.

3. Is it helping me or hurting me?

Again, being super honest with yourself is so important here. If you've made it this far with one of your negative self-talk stories, it's got to be pretty strong. Think about what it's doing to you in the short term and the long. Is it benefiting you over time? Or is it protecting you temporarily from pain? Remember that fear and pain are under all of our negative emotions—*all* of them.

4. What would I say to a friend?

Imagine that your best friends, favorite siblings, or even your colleagues were saying the same things to themselves. What would you say to them, to help them see their assumptions for what they really is? How would you support your friends? What would you do to help your siblings?

My best example of this is my twin boys. As highly sensitive kids, they can both really get down on themselves. When we experience emotional trauma as kids, we internalize it and turn it on ourselves, and my kids are already pretty good at that self-sabotage. When one is down, the other swoops in to help him. After so many years of therapy and a great school that supports emotional intelligence, they've mostly mastered their EQ skills, so they are able to help each other "name it to tame it," experience the sadness or other emotions, and then move on. They give each other the positive talk and the reality check that's necessary when you can't see out of the dark hole you're in. They don't sympathize—they empathize. Both have felt horrible and know how hard it is to see out of the hole, so they can help each other to find the ladder and slowly climb out.

Self-Concept

I've talked a little bit about Kazimierz Dąbrowski, and his Theory of Positive Disintegration, which is about self-concept and how we develop our personalities. Let's go into it a little deeper, with a really lovely metaphor.

Self-concept is what we think of ourselves, and is a reflection of the feedback we've received since birth, from people who played significant roles in our lives. This is the end result of your parents socializing you and sculpting you into the reasonable likeness of what they considered a "good human being." Your parents gave you the yarn to make a sweater and showed you how to knit it. As a gifted person, your experience of the yarn is ... more intense than most. You may see the colors more intensely, or the wool is scratchier for you than it is for others.

Let's think of this in terms of entrepreneurship. You came to this work with a whole truckload of ideas about who you are and why you're doing what you do—this is the amalgamation of ideas, thoughts, concepts, and structure created by your childhood, adulthood, work life, and seeking of rewarding work. You've been socialized to business by your parents and how they got through their day-to-day life, but also by the businesses, leaders, and teachers you've been exposed to, for whatever reason.

You became an entrepreneur as the result of finding all of the other options ... unpalatable.

Maybe you did that as a child, and it's only grown since. Maybe, like me, you came to that as an adult (and somewhat unwillingly). Either way, there was a tension you felt that you couldn't shake off, to be more and do more and break free from the restraints of what you "should be" doing with your life. That is what Dąbrowski called disintegration—that discomfort with how things are going, and the sensation of becoming unraveled.

As you can imagine, once your business personality has been established, it's pretty freaking hard to change it (insert "old dog new tricks" joke here). The way to change it is by receiving new input, new opinions, new feedback, and new socialization that reflects new ideas. With all that newness, it's not shocking that people resist change, is it?

Because it's risky, to willingly go into all that newness, and risk can be *super* scary—particularly if your self-concept is negative, with a heaping of low self-esteem, and sprinkled with impostor syndrome. That's deeper when you're gifted, because you can, if allowed, tend towards over-analysis, tunnel vision, and getting stuck in cycles that are not productive or healthy.

That fear of the unknown can lead to a shutdown. You can become paralyzed with self-doubt and freak out because impostor syndrome is running hog-wild in your brain. Most people think that losing your sh*t like this is bad. We don't want to lose our sh*t because then we look even more unqualified than we already feel, which then leads us even deeper down the rabbit hole of despair. In essence, you put the knitting needles down because you can't handle it right now—and your work starts to unravel.

But what if I told you that what you're seeing as a red flag ("stop what you're doing because you're obviously not going to be successful, and you're wasting everyone's time and no one wants to drink your crappy Kool-Aid anyway") is actually a *green flag*?

That's what Dąbrowski's theory says. When you're feeling unraveled it's because you're getting ready to make a new sweater—you just don't know it. You panic because you only see the unraveling and your instinct is to hold it together at all costs. But just when it feels like your world is falling apart, that's when you've got the best opportunity to make something spectacular. Your unraveling is creating mounds of opportunity to create new stuff that has great potential for being awesome.

Dąbrowski goes even more meta, by

saying that when you're feeling unraveled, it's actually because all this time, you've been knitting a sweater that wasn't even your design! The personality and self-concept you've got has been the design of your parents and all those influential people in your life—who you are when you're at this crossroads is the construct of what other people think you should be. You're a sweater designed by others, not designed by your own self.

How does this play out in your business? You may come to a place in your work where you're stuck and you aren't feeling authentic, and that's maybe being reflected in a lack of sales or a disinterest in being at work, or going through the motions but not getting all the feels you used to from your work.

Can you sit with these feelings? Can you give them space? Can you chill with them and let them mingle in your mind? Now that you've realized you're in a rut and you want to redefine who you are in business and what you are all about, you have an opportunity to create your own personality, with intentionality and authenticity.

When you're in a positive disintegration, you've just realized that the sweater you've got on was knitted by you, but the yarn was given to you by your parents and other influential people in your childhood. When you take control of the development of your sense of self (and in your business), you are creating something new, yet familiar; you're making a new sweater out of old yarn. With that realization, you're suddenly in a yarn store. All the yarn is there for your taking, to create the sweater that is truly yours and authentically you, integrating some (or all) of the yarn from your ravelings, plus new yarn that *you* get to pick out because, dammit, you like it!

You get to do you! Finally!

What yarns will you pick? Do you grab what's right in front of you? Walk around the shop and touch everything? Walk around twice? Three times?

You pick yarns that speak to you, because of their color or their feel, the thickness, or the sparkles (yes, some yarn has sparkles—don't judge). Oh! Maybe you're even eyeing the unspun wool (the stuff that looks like it just came off the sheep or alpaca) and thinking you could needle-felt some elbow patches onto the sweater once it's done. You're thinking about what the sweater will look like when it's done, not just what the yarn looks like in a ball on the shelf.

You're thinking so meta it blows your own damn mind! It's how you roll, my intense friend.

This sweater is you. This sweater is your business (see what I did there). Don't think those are two different sweaters, because that's where people often go wrong. When your personal sweater is expressed in your business, that's when you are the most authentic in your work and that's what clients and customers connect with.

They like the way you knit; they're your

tribe, your peeps, and your network. And that's the awesome sauce. That's the home run.

This is what finding your voice is all about! Since you're reading this book, you're probably on the precipice of that discovery. You're at the doorway of the yarn shop, looking in. By finding your voice, you transform something that might do well at the "ugly sweater" party into a comfy, cute jumper. You get to make that sweater just the way you like it.

Your self-concept defines your values, how you perceive yourself, and how others perceive you. The activities below will help you put those on paper so you can go forward with your most authentic voice.

TIME TO ACT

Now it's time to (begin to) find your own voice. As I mentioned, this chapter will be pretty labor intensive. You're going to need to do a few things (okay, four).

1. Write down your top 10 values (see Appendix C).
2. Do a Myers-Briggs (MB) assessment. They're all over the internet, and they're free or you can pay for one. I think that's silly, so I usually recommend this site for a quick test and a thorough description of the results: https://www.16personalities.com. The assessment is free, but they'll want you to pay for the report. You don't *need* to but you're welcome to if you want to have it on hand. It's the same as what the site tells you, just in a PDF format. The same goes for the Fascination Advantage. Once you're done with that and you read the results, keep in mind that this assessment is preference-based, meaning that your preferences can change. In addition, as has been discussed informally in some communities that I frequent, gifted

individuals can be fairly flexible on some of the questions (mostly because we tend to over-analyze the question).
3. Next, do a Fascination Advantage (FA) assessment. This is one that most people have not heard of, but it is used often by some of the best known and largest companies in the world. Here's that website: http://www.howtofascinate.com.
4. This last step may be more of a leap for some people, but here goes: start a website if you don't already have one. You can make a free one, on WordPress or Wix or SquareSpace, or probably a hundred other websites. Just go find a free WYSIWYG editor and start it up. Do *not* get caught up in design right now. I repeat: do *not* let yourself go down that rabbit hole (it's just a fancy form of procrastination)! This exercise is to help you organize your thoughts

about what you want to say about your business, what you are offering, and how you're going to connect with your audience (blog, Facebook, Twitter, etc.). This is just to start organizing your thoughts, but do start to apply the MB and FA ideas/language.

The chart from Chapter 1 is included here for reference.

Strength	Intensity	Quirk
Produce great services and products	Perfectionism	Can't move on, can't finish
Evaluate all options and see various outcomes	Procrastination	Wait until last minute to complete tasks
Get really deep into subjects when most people only see surface value	Depth	Get tunnel vision and be unable to finish multiple tasks
Asking questions no one else thinks of	Curiosity	Shiny object syndrome, easily distracted
Wide array of skills and educational background	Multi-potentiality	Scattered, jump from job to job

3
Leadership

In my work, I do a lot of research. I read books and blogs, take e-courses, and research business strategy and techniques that other people are teaching. It's one of the tenets of Stephen Covey's book, *The 7 Habits of Highly Effective People* (#7: Sharpen The Saw), but this is also something that I *need* to do. When I'm not learning, I feel a sort of tension in my life. Researching and learning is one of my intensities and it can really wreck me if I either neglect it or I let it get out of control.

When it's moderated, this skill is highly beneficial for me. Not only is it smart in a student-for-life kind of way, but it's proven to be quite useful as a tool for identifying patterns and influences. I can identify the books other people have read, as well as the systems that have influenced their teaching.

Knowing all of this helps me to be a leader of my own stuff because there comes a time when you've done so much research that you finally realize that you've got your stuff sorted. That's the difference between new entrepreneurs and seasoned entrepreneurs – the latter have dealt with their own stuff. They've come to a place of leading others because they've learned how to lead themselves.

The people I study are leaders in their industries, but they're also leaders of their own stuff. They can lead themselves because they've had issues to overcome and then they did just that. These leaders clearly identified their values and principles, and choose to live by them and run their businesses with them in mind. With that said, true leaders don't put all their energetic eggs into one basket. A great leader knows that in order to be the Jedi of their stuff, they need to spread the love – their values are applied to their work, their family, their fun times, and their learning.

They've figured out that they need to focus less on themselves and more on their clients or customers. The seasoned and successful entrepreneur has met their demons and said, "You don't scare me anymore" and can go out into the world confidently helping their clients confront their own demons.

In my opinion, this is the tragic flaw with most life coach training programs: they teach you how to help other people without addressing what's brewing inside first. As Sean Covey says in his book, *The 7 Habits of Highly Effective Teens,* "All change begins with you ... Succeeding with yourself always comes before succeeding with other people."

Great leaders are making choices every day about what they can accept and what they reject. We can't accept everything, because then we stand for nothing; when we reject nothing, we succumb to shiny object syndrome. We develop our personality and our self-concept based on what we accept or reject. Why do you need to define and set intention with leadership in your business? One word: focus. You can't build a brand when you're standing for nothing, are scattered in your thinking, and have no solid idea of your self-concept.

But when you make solid decisions about what you will reject in your business, you gain clarity about what you stand for and what makes you unique. Finding that clarity is what helps potential clients understand if they like you. Do you resonate with them? Do you reject and accept the same ideals and values that they do? Finding clarity about the values you cannot accept in your business is going to get you closer to finding the focus that you need.

I want to talk about two types of focus. There's the focus you place on your clients, in terms of sorting out issues, like I mentioned above; if you're still working on your own issues, you're not going to be able to help your clients as effectively. And then there's the focus you have in your business, in leading yourself, which is what you need clarity on before you can turn the focus onto your clients. That's the leading-yourself kind of focus.

When you lack focus in self-leadership, you are not headed in one direction; the distractions come at you at warp speed and you can't resist the shiny objects. When you lack focus, you're confused, and as Beth Buelow says, in her book (*The Introvert Entrepreneur*), "A confused mind always says no." When you're confused about what you're doing and why you're doing it, that is translated to your clients. Your clients and customers can't say yes to your business when they're confused about what you do and why you do it.

But when you have focus—oh my! The possibilities! When you have focus, you have clarity and can easily commit to your decisions. Your passion shows through and you make it your every day practice to infuse it into everything you do. Your clients and customers see it and feel it when you're clear and focused. They want what you've got to offer, when you're focused. As the leader of your business, you express that focus in your values, your self-concept, and your authentic voice. When you're leading yourself, you're deeply in touch with what you're doing and why you do it, and that's super shiny to your clients. You can tell them, with authority, why you are the solution to their problems.

When you're focused in your business, it gives you the freedom to say no to distractions, which allows you the time, space, and brain space to concentrate on the parts of your business that need attention. These bits and pieces are important because what you pay attention to, grows. You water the plants, and they grow; you don't, and they die (let's assume we're talking about ferns here, not cacti). When you pay attention, you're open to opportunities to grow those bits and pieces.

Another great TED talker, Simon Sinek, talks about "people don't buy what you do, they buy why you do it." Leadership, in this context, begins with inspiration, and gut reactions. The best way to connect with clients is to reach their emotions, and great leaders know that. Great leaders want to inspire you first, to connect their beliefs with your beliefs, and to reach the most basic part of your brain— — your actions are the tangible evidence of what you believe. That's resonance, and that's what clients connect with.

Transformational Leadership

There are a number of leadership styles, including authoritarian, paternalistic, democratic, laissez-faire, transactional, and transformational. The most growth comes from being a transformational leader because that is the leader who can use all the leadership styles and techniques *in the appropriate situation at the appropriate time.* If you are any of the other types of leaders, 100% of the time, you will experience less success because the other types are too extreme. When you're a transformational leader, you are an artist using different paints to create a body of work that is the expression of your values and your voice. Transformational leaders get greater results and have more impact, with a far greater reach in their influence. As you can probably see, leadership is an art and it's definitely one of those times when you recognize it but struggle to define it from scratch.

Leadership is knowing when to use the right skills at the right time. Sometimes you have to practice tough love and be a hardass, while other times you have to be more compassionate and easygoing. Some circumstances call for perseverance, and others call for a pivot. Being a transformational leader is knowing when to use which technique in the occasion that calls for it. As with so many things in life, you get better at that with experience. Making decisions trains you and your brain in how to make more (better) decisions.

In leading yourself in your organization, you must be objective (while being the subject), passionate (while being disconnected enough to pass on your great ideas that aren't going to get you anywhere), and inspiring (but not facilitating your own co-dependent issues). You are a goal-setter with high expectations, but can have compassion and flexible thinking when you've not met those goals. You have to make solid commitments and then follow through with them.

For the intense entrepreneur, probably the hardest part of leading yourself in your business is knowing when your intensities are getting in your way. Being fully aware and honest with yourself is the kryptonite to that, but it's easier said than done. Perfectionism, procrastination, and rabbit-holing (yep, made that a verb just now) are all signs that you're getting in your own way, and holding up your own progress. Knowing when your intensities are getting out of hand will be very important for you.

Reverse-Engineering Leadership

Did you know that, because gifted and intense people are very good at metacognition, it makes us superstars at reverse-engineering? We see overall pictures quickly and thoroughly, but sometimes fall short with filling in the details. When you're seeing the world from 10,000 feet, it's hard to even see those little ant details that make up the big picture.

But reverse-engineering is your weapon of choice here. You can see the 10,000-foot view, so let's back-track until we can get the details broken down to manageable pieces. You know a good leader when you see one. You know who you want to follow because they have … something special. Let's break down what they've got going on so you can see how to develop those skills in leading yourself in your business. Because, let's face it, as an entrepreneur, you are both investor and investee in terms of human capital development.

When you're working for yourself, no one is in charge of you, but if you don't work with focus and intention, the whole thing can fall apart. Or at the very least, you will lose (or lack) momentum and seem scattered; clients pick up on that, so finding focus extends outward in your communications, and through leadership.

Leadership in entrepreneurship is important because you can't just drift along, throwing spaghetti at the wall and waiting to see what will stick. That's not leadership. As discussed previously, you have to be a scientist, the head scientist, and experimentation is fine as long as you have methodology, intention, and your Chief Initiative in mind (at the very front of your brain, not malingering in the back corners).

Systems Thinking

In *The Fifth Discipline*, Peter Senge talks about how systems thinking integrates pretty much everything we've talked about so far. I'm paraphrasing here, to put his ideas into my own voice, but the initial four disciplines are:

- Your personal vision or Chief Initiative
- Visualization, and getting over assumptions and thinking in terms of perspectives
- The reflection of your community as a mirror of your most authentic voice
- Open thinking by accepting other input besides your own

Systems thinking is the fifth discipline and it integrates all of those ideas and acknowledges that they are a system, not independent of each other. They work together to create a transformational leadership profile that is open to change and uses flexible thinking at every opportunity. Systems thinking will give you the ability to reverse-engineer your leadership style.

You are part of many systems, which include your family, your church or other organizations you participate in, your work, and your school. There is overlap with these systems, and they all affect each other. The system you create as an entrepreneur is a standalone but doesn't have to be a silo.

As a great leader in your system, you need various qualities to be successful. These are the qualities you admire in others. They include: initiative, grit, the ability to inspire others, firm (focused) decision-making, the ability to ask for help and collaborate when necessary, humility, and also pride. Obviously this is not an exhaustive list, but you can see that leadership is a matter of balance, choices, and flexibility.

Design Thinking

Another construct, design thinking, has 6 aspects that you need to bounce between: understand, observe, point of view, ideate, prototype, test, and iterate. The gist of design thinking is that you are thinking from your customer/client's perspective, listening to their ideas, being creative and innovative in how you design your products/services to meet their needs, and problem-solving along the way to be sure that iterations are optimized.

The leader who utilizes design thinking is being empathetic, open minded, nonjudgmental, and holistic. It should be obvious that this type of leader is also optimistic, curious, and looks for learning opportunities in failures.

When you're a design-thinking leader in your entrepreneurial entity, you're doing all of that, and it's driven by your values. If your values clash with your leadership style, you're not going to get very far. You will seek and listen intently to feedback from your clients or customers, iterate, and move on.

TIME TO ACT

1. Write down your values. Yes, you did this for the last chapter, I just want you to re-write them to highlight what you really believe in and what you're doing.

2. Now write down what you *don't* stand for. What will you not accept in your business? — what values do you reject?

3. Describe the leadership qualities you feel will make you a great leader. Show how you will put these into practice in your daily work.

4
Networking for the Intense Entrepreneur

Although there are plenty of gifted and intense extroverts, I don't typically hear from them that they suffer from networking. It is most likely a problem if you are an introvert, and it has the potential to be torture. It can feel awkward, anxiety-producing, and/or soul crushing. Networking can be noisy, confusing, overwhelming, and it will drain your energy like a sleep-deprived toddler on a sugar high. It can be all of those things, at various stages and degrees—or none. You're in control, so you get to decide how it will go. I'll just come right out and tell you that avoidance is not a strategy; instead of avoiding what doesn't work, you will need to find what *does* work for you and optimize it.

Don't fret. With awareness and strategy, you can get the best out of networking. First and foremost, you'll need to reframe how you think about networking. Is introversion part of yourself that you consider to be a flaw? Read anything by Susan Cain, Lisa Petrilli, or Beth Buelow and you'll realize that being an introvert does not have to be a flaw—it has the ability to be your superpower. Reframe it to be just that. Engage your vivid imagination to see what it would be like to prepare for, work through a networking event, and then reward yourself for surviving.

Part of the reframing is thinking about

the impact you want to have. Who are you trying to reach, and what is the impact you want to have on them? What results do you want them to experience? This reframing is the setup for going into any networking event because it helps you switch the focus off of you and onto your client (the reason you're there).

When you think of a networking event as a way to make business contacts, it starts to feel scary. It can feel like, if you aren't successful, your business may suffer. But if you can reframe to think of it as giving your services to the world, you'll be able to see it differently. You may be thinking that this perspective borders on arrogance. It can if you're a jerk about it. But if you are able to see yourself as having truly valuable services that help people, you can change that point of view. If you truly believe in your services and the benefits to others, and connect with the emotions of that impact, you'll be well on your way to a great (altruistic) mindset, and your business will reflect that.

After reframing, you'll need to get strategic—you need a plan that works for you, in most situations. It won't always be feasible, but with a strategy in place, you can make do when you're thrown a curveball. I've found the most effective strategy involves not just planning for the event itself, but planning for the before and the after.

Pre-Event

How can you best prepare for an event? No matter what it is, a group event, a meeting with a single person who is a big influencer, or some other gathering, you've usually got an opportunity to prepare (and you can plan the prep time into your strategy). I personally try to avoid any situation where I can't prepare before hand, but that's not always possible. If you can prepare, you will feel more confident and be able to handle it better.

Your intense drive to research can be your best friend in networking. I like to research (part of the intellectual OE) my subject as much as possible, so that I'm able to have an intelligent conversation. I research the people talking or the major influencers in the group, the subjects they're talking about or their favorite projects, and the big ideas that are being proposed. If that feels too big, you can break it down into more bite-sized pieces.

Research and practice will help you feel better about networking events because you'll be a little bit ahead of the game (as opposed to going in unprepared). Practice what you can, to help overcome much of the spotlight anxiety (for example, rehearse your speech, practice your elevator pitch, and/or repeat your achievements to yourself).

Another aspect of work you can do ahead of the event is to practice self-compassion (you should also do this during and afterward; heck, you should practice this *all* the time!). When you can go into a situation thinking about being human, knowing you'll make mistakes, and having realistic expectations, you'll be better equipped to deal with what lies ahead.

And my final strategy for pre-networking events comes from Amy Cuddy's book, *Presence*. In the book, she talks about power posing and its effect on your confidence and personal power. I highly recommend her TED talk and her book, but until you've watched/read, think of powerful poses (imagine Superman or Wonder-Woman), and strike that pose for a few minutes before you go into a networking event. This is an incredibly useful technique that can help you whether you're the keynote speaker or an audience member.

Working the Networking (During-Event)

Part of the reason introverts hate networking is because we feel like we're put on the spot, then can't speak coherently and make fools of ourselves. Reframing networking means consciously taking the spotlight off yourself and putting it on someone else (in a complimentary way), listening intensely (is there any other way?), and making your conversational companion feel like the only person in the room.

Have you ever watched live coaching, where a coach is on a stage, doing their talk, and then they invite an audience member to be coached live and on the spot? Anthony Robbins is *great* at this. He has audience members stand up and tell why they're there or ask the question they want answered. Then he digs in—and it's almost magical to watch. He will turn people inside out and upside down by being super curious, and they leave with their lives changed. They experience instant transformation, which is *extremely* valuable. If you tune into what he's doing, he's asking them why, why, why, and why, to get down to the real depth of their pain. He goes to the absolute foundation of their suffering, which is raw and scary for the subject. He is curious and digs deep; he listens to verbal responses and observes non-verbal cues. Then he makes them stars by showing them how they're human and honest and real—and that it's okay to be that way. He takes away their shame, forgives them, and forces them to forgive themselves—on the spot! How powerful is that?

In less than ten minutes he can change audience members' entire perspective, and it's long-lasting change because it was so vivid, real, and (let's be honest here) scary. In that short time period, he turned the attention on his guests, listened intently, and made them stars. Those are super skills that he's mastered, and you can, too, with practice and intention. He uses his curiosity and knowledge of human nature to optimize his interactions.

The way you show up for your event or your clients should always be in your most authentic voice—even if you're not talking. When you show up wondering what you can get out of the interaction, you're doing yourself and your client/audience a disservice. When you show up wondering how you can be of service, you're going to be way ahead of the game.

Show up with your intensities beaming. You're super curious, so use that to ask questions and take the spotlight off yourself. You're a great listener, so use that to really (truly) hear what people are saying around you. Listen for your cue to the conversation – and if there never is one, then you've done a lot to listen and add to your body of research. The point here is to use your intensities to your advantage.

Post-Event

After you've survived, you should first think about what you learned at the event and jot down notes; second, you should definitely reward yourself with whatever you need to feel rewarded.

You can always figure out *something* you learned from the event, even if that lesson is that you don't like to go to events like that. But if you can start the event knowing that you're going to need to take down some notes afterward, you'll be more aware during the event itself.

What do you need to feel rewarded? A night at a posh hotel all on your own? Yes. Or maybe a bowl of ice cream on the couch in your sweats with Netflix and some knitting? Abso-freaking-lutely! If you're an extrovert, this may be going out with friends to celebrate. Find your reward, and plan it out along with planning the event itself. This is essential because networking can drain your energy and knowing how to re-supply that energy is going to be key to your not dreading the next event.

Gifted and intense people use energy as currency, so losing it can really cost you time and productivity the following day (or week), or in other ways, like in relationships. Having a way to intentionally refuel yourself is the key to being able to do it again some other day. Plan to be "out of office" for one to three days after an event; just take a few days off to recover and nurture yourself. You'll dread the event less, it will become a positive story in your self-talk, and it will be part of your new perspective on networking.

Don't forget your post-event super-size dose of self-compassion!

Overall

Now think about your networking advantages. What do you do really well that translates into a superpower in these situations? You're probably a great listener, which is a huge bonus. You likely have excellent skills in researching, and that is also helpful. Could you team up in a collaborative relationship with an extrovert (more on collaborations in Chapter 6)?

Everyone defines networking differently. Some people do most of it on social media. Others form support groups to create the infrastructure for networking. Some people actually love going to conferences and summits. How do you define networking? What is the ideal situation for you to meet and talk with potential customers or clients? Does networking for you consist of connecting with people one-on-one and not in a group? What about one-on-one within a group?

If you can take the initiative and reach out to one person in a large group, you've basically temporarily eliminated all the other people in the room because now you can focus on just one.

TIME TO ACT

Think of a time when you were really great at some networking event or some way that you gained a lot of subscribers, followers, or clients. What happened before, during, and after that event? How can you systematize and optimize that?

Run through this with a number of situations. It doesn't have to be professional. It could be a personal thing, like a family

Christmas party or other family gathering that went really well, or a friend's BBQ. You'll need to pick out and identify the characteristics of what occurred so that you can try to reproduce them. Your strategy will consist of your networking advantages, your definition of the ideal networking situation for you (look at Appendix C for a list of suggestions), and the characteristics of a smooth networking operation.

Now that you have a solid picture in your head of what it looks like to have success in networking, you're going to describe your strategies. You should have two strategies: one for networking events (an event strategy), and one for reaching out to network in a non-event-centered way (an ongoing strategy). They should both incorporate methods of using your intensities to optimize your experience and your efforts.

1. Event Strategy

The event strategy will be your plan on

how to tackle structured events with multiple people. It will be your plan for not just surviving, but thriving in a networking situation. Use the description in this chapter as your springboard for inspiration. Describe, in detail, your before- during- and post-event plan for optimizing events to your best advantage, and using your intensities as your strengths.

2. Ongoing Strategy

The ongoing strategy will be your plan on how to continue nurturing relationships so that your clients don't drop out of your system. Use the list of possible connections in Appendix C for your inspiration here. This should also include a time-sensitive quality to it. For example, if you want to reach people one-on-one, could you commit to reaching out to five different people via phone, email, or social media once per week? Create a schedule for re-evaluation, modification, and iteration of your ongoing strategy for connection.

Once you have mapped out your strategies, give them a try. Go out and experiment. Try out your plan and be observant. Keep a close eye on what works and what doesn't. Do it in multiple situations, because just doing it once isn't a good sample size. You'll need a respectable sample size in order to draw conclusions about causation. You'll also need to work at it for a bit of time in order to have a large enough sample size (a week isn't really enough to figure out if you're connecting with people through your blog or your newsletter).

5
Sales and Marketing

Sales and marketing are likely some of the most avoided and despised pieces of entrepreneurship among my clients. They don't like self-promotion, feel like they're being a bother to people, or just have an icky feeling.

The difference between sales and marketing is that sales is primarily transactional, whereas marketing is an overall blanket for all of what you do. Sales is the experience of working with you, and actually hiring you. Marketing is your brand, the feel of your business, and why you do what you do. They overlap quite a bit, especially in a small business, but they should both convey your personality and your values.

When you know your message and you're in touch with your authentic voice, you can feel good about sales and marketing because it's no longer sales and marketing—it's informing people about who you are, what you do, and how it will change their lives. You truly believe in your product or service, and you're conveying the experience of working with you or owning your item.

You may need to switch your mindset of selling to something that more closely resembles a way to create and amplify value. Your product won't help your client if they don't see or feel the value in it. The way to get there is marketing, which is the connection between your client's problems and your solution.

One last thing about sales and marketing—your strategies here should not be trying to convince potential clients of your qualifications. Rather, you should be conveying value. If you have to convince someone you're the one, it means they're already looking for ways to disqualify you (ways you'll disappoint them), and you fall into that trap when you struggle to use your voice to talk about how qualified you are. Instead, you want to communicate the value of your offerings.

What is the value to your client? What transformation will they experience from working with you? Transformation is value, and your sales and marketing need to convey the value that they're looking for, so that your message resonates with them.

Sales

No matter what industry you're in, you're going to have to make your presence known in a complex and overwhelming world that already has *way* too many choices. You do that by using your authentic voice, in your most comfy networking platforms, and you're going to do it with ease when you realize that you're a natural salesperson.

Many training programs on sales out there will try to tell you to *show the why* and *sell the how*—but this is *so* wrong. People don't just buy because you have the answers to their problems. Ultimately, they can just Google it, so you're kind of selling yourself short (and underestimating your potential customer/client) if you think you're the only one out there with a solution to their problems. They will buy the *why* of what you do, once they figure out what it is they want. You have an opportunity to tell them what they want/need and then be the *only* solution.

People buy for a variety of reasons, but having an emotional connection to your solution is going to have you ahead of the game. In his TED talk and book, Simon Sinek says that people don't buy *what* you do, they buy *why* you do it. They buy your experience and your knowledge; they buy to be held accountable to themselves; they buy as a means of going deeper into what they already want; they buy as a way to access you and your feedback.

The Funnel of Engagement

In her book, *The Introvert Entrepreneur,* Beth Buelow outlines a five-step process for changing your perspective on sales (see below). You need to help clients and prospects progress from *know* to *like* to *trust,* and as they do, they will get closer and closer to converting into paying customers.

1. Reframing—the way you think of sales is apparent when you deal with your clients and customers. Show up the way you want to be perceived. When you stop thinking you're a used car salesman, you won't be perceived that way.

2. Why people say no—there are a lot of reasons, but consider that there are a few key points here: they can't (or won't) buy if

they don't *know* you exist, if they don't *like* you and your message, or if they don't *trust* you.

3. Why-How-What—no one will say yes to you if you aren't clear about what you have to offer. Know your values, know your Chief Initiative, and be able to convey what you offer clearly and succinctly.

4. Don't rush—go slow and create space for people to make a decision about you and your services. Take plenty of time to demonstrate or illustrate the experience for them.

5. Repeat—you can't do this once and expect results. You're going to have to do this work constantly. Experiment along the way, as long as it is methodical and measured, so you know what techniques are having the impact you are looking for.

It is essential to note that this process is ongoing. You don't just do it when you're at an ebb in your business—you have to do sales and marketing in both ebb and flow, because you're cultivating relationships and that takes time.

Like you, your clients are more likely to buy from a referral from a friend before they buy from a random service provider. The funnel of engagement is the process flow of cultivating relationships, and can be used for nonprofits, businesses, and any other organization that cares about how the stakeholders are cultivated (everyone should care about that!).

In my work with nonprofits, I saw the funnel work like this: someone is interested in the mission of the nonprofit and decides to donate a small amount. They then decide to volunteer because they want to make a difference. As they get more ingrained in the culture and mission, they start to donate funds. If that relationship is properly cultivated, they donate more money over time, and then want to be part of the decision-making process of where their money goes and how it is spent. That's when they join the board of directors, where they can be part of the decision-making process and they will be the ultimate fans (and thus donate more money).

Similar to nonprofit board members, sales aren't made in a one-time exchange. That would be like asking someone to marry you in the first five minutes you've known them. It's a whole conversation, a cultivated and nurtured relationship.

Your clients should progress naturally in a similar fashion, through their own motivation and interest in your message and products. How they progress is partly human nature and partly your actions.

There are six qualities that psychologist Robert Cialdini identifies in his book, *Influence: The Psychology of Persuasion*, as the human nature aspect of persuasion: reciprocity (people are more likely to buy if they've been given something of value first), commonality (also referred to as resonance; people want to feel like you have something in common with them, that you get them), authority (that there is evidence of your competence—not necessarily in degrees or certifications), social proof (people want to go with the herd, no matter how different they think they are), scarcity (the fewer opportunities available, the more likely they are to feel like they "need" to buy), and consistency (your message needs to be the same throughout your campaigns; this is how you build trust).

These qualities should be evident in your marketing and sales. Here's an example of how it might play out for you, with the quality addressed in parentheses:

- Offers freebies on the website (reciprocity and commonality).

- Blogs one or two times per week (authority and consistency, also reciprocity in the form of free advice).

- Has website content that is of value to readers (landing page, sales page, blog, etc.) addresses issues that clients face (commonality).

- Testimonials are scattered throughout website (social proof and authority, as well as commonality).

- Sales page demonstrates limited opportunities for one-on-one engagement (scarcity).

- Everything about you, your website, your social media strategies, and your other content should convey the same message and character, but you should also be reliable and responsible with your communications with clients (consistency).

If your message telling them why you do what you do is clear and authentic, they will organically progress their way down the funnel, from ToFu to MoFu to BoFu and into the Promoter category (see descriptions below). This is the *know-like-trust* progression.

ToFu (Top of Funnel)—Learners in a phase of awareness, getting to *know* your business. They want helpful, relevant info, and are looking for solutions. Your keywords (SEO) and blog content, as well as other forms of social media, are the best way to connect with this group, which makes up about 85% of your total traffic. People at this stage see your Kool-Aid stand.

MoFu (Middle of Funnel)—Shoppers in a consideration phase, thinking about trying your biz out; they *like* what they see in you. They want options, make educated decisions, and are looking for offers (value). Your best way to connect with this group will be reviews, case studies, and blog posts with solutions for problems described clearly, with a strong and convenient call-to-action. This group makes up about 10% of your total traffic. People at this stage think your Kool-Aid looks yummy.

BoFu (Bottom of Funnel)—Buyers in a decision phase; they want to buy your products/services because they *trust* you. They evaluate the quality of service you provide and your value to them, specifically. Product demos, samples, free trials, consults, and "buy now" options are great ways to connect with this group. This group makes up about 5% of your total traffic. People at this stage want to buy your Kool-Aid.

When they come out of BoFu, they are customers who are likely to become promoters—if you keep nurturing the relationship. You can't stop cultivating the relationship just because they buy a product. They will sell your business for you and be part of your marketing team, by telling their friends about you and referring others. People at this stage will sell your Kool-Aid to everyone they know.

Of course, any person visiting your website, blog, Twitter account, Instagram account, etc. can become promoters and transition through these stages. Your job is to advance them forward (with their permission!) and provide content that reaches each one of them, so that they *want* to progress. Referrals come from promoters, and you want as many of those as you can get, because they do your advertising for you. Automation is your helper in moving people along the funnel. Every potential client has the potential to transition through the whole funnel. They're on a continuum, not fixed points. (Note that permission is super important in this process because you can't sell your product or service to someone who doesn't want it; when a client gives you permission to contact them (by subscribing to your newsletter, for example), they are saying they want to hear what you have to say).

Think about a sales conversation going like this (think about a great sale or exchange in the past):

- Start by asking about the problems and challenges your potential clients face.
- Next, illuminate the connections between those problems and your unique solution.

- Add some expert insight—your special sauce that you add.

- Then, ask about their goals and hopes. Keep asking why to really get to the root of why they want what they want—then tell them even more is possible. Channel your inner Tony Robbins. Get down to the really basic emotions.

- Provide some insight for why they haven't reached their goal yet. Offer some suggestions of how to overcome their specific challenges.

At this point, they're going to be ready to buy.

Marketing

Popular opinion right now is that you have anywhere from seven to twelve seconds to capture the attention of visitors to your website. That's insane, but I'm sure you know why it is so small. The world we're living in is overwhelming in volume and there's no time to focus before you get distracted by the next article or website. That's not much time to get your whole story across, so you'd better find a way to connect with viewers' emotions almost immediately.

I heard a really super example of this the other day on a commercial that I couldn't exit out of on the internet (so annoying). The commercial was for a minivan. Marketers in the automotive industry have really grown out of the utilitarian mindset and into the mind-space of parents. It didn't talk about the features of the van, like the functionality of the captain's chairs in the second row, the square footage of interior space, or the air conditioning.

Instead, the commercial talked about the ease of use when you put your baby's car seat into that second row captain's chair, all the stuff you can get into the back of the van when you take your son to college for the first time, and the relief of having a cool car for your daughter when you're taking her to the church on her wedding day. This car manufacturer really got to the heart of the emotions at each one of those events, and how the functions of the car will always be there for the owners. They conveyed luxury, ease of use, and flexibility through emotions. Jeez, that's *good*!

Here's another example: Compare a baker who makes bread and doesn't do any branding or marketing, with a baker who sells the love and friendship associated with sharing a meal with your friends and family, and at the center of the table is a loaf of her bread from which everyone tears a piece off. See how the latter is going to sell more?

Emotions are at the center of marketing, whether you're using positive emotions or negative (see anything written by Seth Godin for further research on this). An example of using negative emotions in marketing is the "fear of missing out." It even has an acronym (FOMO). I'm not a huge fan of doom and gloom tactics, but there are some good points with this logic. I think most of us want to avoid using this tactic because we don't want people to feel bad about coming to us or our products, but it doesn't have to be like that. When you're using your personal style, and it attracts your type of clients, you're already filtering out the people who can't use your service, don't want what you have to sell, or aren't a good fit. You should not neglect the sense that they want to avoid more losses, avoid feeling ineffective, avoid feeling alone, and avoid feeling like they or their product is no longer necessary.

How can you connect with the emotions of what it will be like to buy from you or use your services? What is it like to work with you? How can you convey that experience to your audience when they aren't in your presence? You have a story to tell, and you need to have a deep understanding of how your story resonates with your audience—is it a story that is true and a story they want to share? That resonance is the key to your sales strategy.

Your story

The first part of marketing is figuring out your message, your story the you want to tell. It should express your authentic voice, and you can use the work from Chapters 1 and 2 as a guide. Your MB and FA will give you the language to get started with telling the story of who you are, as a business.

Channels

Next is determining what medium to use to communicate it. In the appendix you will see a list of some ideas for reaching clients, but it is not exhaustive. Get creative here! You can certainly come up with your own methods or combinations of methods for reaching your audience. But the list is a good place to start.

Measurable outcomes (aka data)

So you take your voice, get it out by the channels you choose, and then what? You need to know if it's working. How will you measure success? And how will you price your services or products?

Google measures its success by how little time Googlers spend on their website. Success to them is someone leaving their website. If you think about it, it makes total sense. They help you find stuff, so if you find what you're looking for and leave, they've done their job. Success. Figure out what success is to you. What will you measure?

Pricing

When you go into developing a marketing plan for your business, you are going to need to figure out your pricing. Keep in mind that you're not going to charge merely what it costs to make or provide something. You're charging based on what your product or service is *worth*, which includes the cost of production, your time, your profit, and your experience. When you take all of that into account, you get a real idea of your value.

One day Picasso was in a coffee shop and a waitress saw him doodling on a napkin, and when he was done, she asked if she could buy it from him. He said sure, and that the price was $20,000. She was shocked and remarked on how it took him 20 minutes to doodle on a napkin, why would it cost so much? He said, "No, it's taken me 20 years to create this." This story was greatly paraphrased, but the point here is that you're not charging for what it takes to make or the hour of your time. You're charging for everything that has gone into your product or service—your college degrees, the books you've read, the conferences you've attended, every single phone call and email that you've sent/received in correspondence to establish your product. This is *all* part of the value, and it's a reflection of how you feel about your product or service. Charge appropriately.

When you think of messages and marketing, remember to be open-minded, think of alternatives, and really consider the marketing tools utilized by industries other than the one you're in. Oftentimes, strategies that are commonly used in another industry can be shockingly innovative in your own.

Logic Model

Logic models are used in the nonprofit world as a tool for keeping your initiatives easy to access and checking for progress, but I love using them in business because it's a great way to visualize your business and to make sure that your values are evident throughout your processes. This tool outlines your input, activities, output, and outcomes, as well as data collection methods and indicators of the outcomes.

Input—What you put into your business; includes time, money, resources, and anything outside entities put into your business (e.g., $/mo in overhead, time per week spending time with clients, time per week blogging, etc.)

Activities—What your business does (e.g., coaching, producing gadgets, giving some sort of service, etc.)

Output—What you can measure (e.g., # products sold in a day, # clients per month, etc.)

Outcome—What you want your clients/customers to do or feel after having used your business (e.g., entrepreneurs will be more clear and focused, so that they can get more clients and make more money).

Data Collection—What will you use to measure your effectiveness? What numbers are representative of your impact?

Indicators—What will be your sign of success? (ex. # of successful clients making X amount of dollars more per year as a result of working with me, # of happy customers in one year, etc.).

For the visual-spatial learner, this tool

is helpful because it is so easily used in a visual representation. Google it, and you'll see many brightly colored logic models showing the reason organizations do what they do—it puts your "why" on display so you can see it clearly. It is meant to be a picture of your ideal business.

TIME TO ACT

Sales Strategy

Your sales strategy should do all of the following:

- Communicate the problem your potential client faces
- Empathize with that problem—make a connection
- Tell why you do what you do
- Describe how what you do is the solution to the client's problem
- Incorporate your intensities as your strengths

Describe, in detail, the above items and indicate where each item should be included in your marketing (sales page, blog, home page, etc.).

Marketing Strategy

Using your values, MB and FA, write down the message you want to convey.

Pick some channels to use to reach your audience (look at Appendix C for a list of suggestions).

Adjust your website, blog, emails, newsletters, etc. to reflect your message. Your character and personality should shine through in everything you do.

Pick some measurable data to gauge whether your strategy is working.

Take note of how your intensities can help/hinder here. This is a place where people often go astray, by measuring the data that's not relevant, and then fixating on it. Make sure you're using ideas here that work to support your sub-goals, and, ultimately, your Chief Initiative.

Logic Model
Create a logic model for your business using the descriptions from the chapter. Make sure it demonstrates your values. For example, if creativity is one of your top values, your Activities should reflect a sense of artistic expression and your flavor of creativity.

6
Community

By now you may realize that a great way to cultivate the relationships you have with your potential clients and customers is in a community. Creating a sense of community surrounding your business can greatly increase your brand's value because a community fosters a sense of belonging and a platform for resonance. It feels so good to know that others have had similar experiences, similar taste, and similar goals. It's validating, when you've spent your whole life thinking you were somehow broken, didn't fit in, didn't get along, and were "too much" for most people.

Gathering is what we want naturally, whether gifted or not, and the online world is making it possible to gather virtually with people around the globe. That is SO awesome. I really love it. Facebook is full of groups that support one or more of the characteristics of giftedness. Likewise, there are groups all over the place to support entrepreneurship, art work, knitting, website design, etc. The goal of all of these communities is to bring like-minded people together. Some are monetized (charge for membership) and some are not. Either way, they are creating value for the members.

Some possible ways of cultivating community as a means of providing a place for you to support your customers/clients include: email, blogging, social media, webinars, in-person gatherings, mastermind groups, public speaking, and even creating your own online space for groups to congregate virtually (such as membership communities). See appendix C for more examples.

No matter what medium you choose, your interactions in your community should be consistent, reliable, authentic, and helpful. That is what creates the value for your followers and subscribers. They're looking for access to you and your advice, products, and personality because that's how they feel connected. That connection is their sense of resonance, which translates to transformation and value.

The way you show up for these relationships will dictate how it evolves. Show up with an open mind, a respectful attitude, and a curious mind, and you will likely do well. With that said, honesty is probably one of the biggest keys to collaborative relationships. If there are trust issues between you and your co-collaborator, they can be extremely difficult, if not impossible, to overcome. The flip side of that is being too honest, which can happen frequently with gifted people who can be laser-focused on the goal and not terribly concerned with the etiquette of how to get there. There is a lot to be said for using a healthy dose of tact with your honesty.

Collaboration

Collaboration is one way of creating a sense of community. Let's start with an example here, as a means of description.

Let's say you want to build a community for your artistic services. You sell art (photography, paintings, knitted hats, whatever), and you realize that creating a community will help foster good feelings about your products. It's a way for your clients to be in contact with you and perhaps learn your techniques or your philosophy. You could create a Facebook group or a login membership community on your website.

Next you'll want to bring in other experts to help support your community. In this example, you may collaborate with website designers so that you have that type of support for your members. You could also collaborate with marketing experts, to help your members learn how to market their artwork. By collaborating, you're creating a deeper relationship with your members and giving them more value.

There are a variety of ways to collaborate and work with others, even though you're an independent practitioner. When considering these types of relationships, you will do well to plan, as much as possible, for any and all outcomes. You can do this by knowing your co-collaborator well before you change the relationship, working out the details in a legal document if necessary, and understanding how each party will deal with conflict. With proper planning, you can be hugely successful.

If you can see your business being amplified by another business or by a colleague, or even if you're just wanting to work with someone you admire — those are both good reasons to collaborate. There are many forms of collaboration, including accountability partners, advisors, and like-minded businesses.

An alternative form of collaboration is to form a strategic alliance. Can your organization and another one help each other out? Maybe you can reach an audience that they can't, and vice versa; or maybe you have services that they don't have the infrastructure to provide. These types of relationships can be very beneficial for all parties, but please, do your due diligence! Make sure you've studied them, their beliefs and actions, and what people say about them. When you form an alliance like this, you're taking on their reputation and they're taking on yours. Make sure you're a good fit, including your values and goals.

Another form of collaboration, and one of my personal favorites, is coaching. Coaches don't just tell you what to do; they work with you, in a balanced relationship, to work towards the goals that you define.

It's a pretty fun experience, and can do wonders for your business. Trust me.

Yet another is consulting (also one of my favorites). When you consult, you're asking someone else to solve your problem and you go into it with an open mind and a humble attitude. If you consult with me to help your organization, you need to be able to do what I tell you to do. You can trust that consultants have your best interest in mind because when you succeed, it's a sign of their success. That's one way that consulting and coaching are similar.

TIME TO ACT

1. Describe your plan for creating a sense of community in for your business, including answering the following questions. What methods of connection will you use? How will you create value in your community? How will you measure success in your community? Will you include strategic or other collaborations?

7
Iteration and Sustainability

Iteration and sustainability are both things you should think of from the beginnings of your business. If you haven't thought of planning for these, don't worry—it's not too late. What most people don't realize is that *never* considering them can hold your business back.

If you want your business to go viral, you have to think like a virus. A disease that spreads quickly does less damage than one that settles in and spreads slowly, creeping through the masses. In this context, the "damage" is the impact of your business on your clients and their work, and the reach of your influence. Is your business going to spread fast and then be forgotten, or stick around and be talked about in the long term, adapting and spreading slowly but surely until it conquers the world?

Iteration is the process of evolving your products into new products. For example, your coaching can become a course, your coaching course can become a self-paced e-course, and then you can write a book (about the course or about the process of iteration or course development). The possibilities are endless. These different iterations also serve the purpose of supporting each other. The book serves as a promoter of the course, the course serves as a promoter of your one-on-one coaching, etc.

In addition, your potential clients are on a bell curve, with early adopters hopping in at the beginning (want only new stuff, and give in to shiny object syndrome at the drop of a hat), the masses in the middle, and the laggards at the opposite end (they don't adopt easily, don't like change, and don't like new stuff). Your process of iteration can serve each of these groups. Early adopters want a new and fresh product, whereas laggards want a stable and time-tested product. You'll need to create products that targets which types of clients you are aiming for. Do you want the people who only buy new and shiny? Or the masses that buy stability? Either is fine, just make that decision from the get-go. You can always pivot if it's not working out.

Sustainability

What will your business look like in ten years? Considering the answer to this question will help to gauge your commitment, but also your conceptual vision of sustainability. Was your answer anything that resembles, "I don't know"? If so, you'd better think long and hard about what you're doing here and why you're doing it.

One thing I've noticed is that what you pay attention to will grow; if you neglect it, it will wither. If there are parts (or big chunks) of your business that you're neglecting, they will eventually die or whither. Make sure, from the beginning, that you're thinking of the long-term sustainability and acting with intention.

To be sustainable, you'll need to be sure your planning is structured for the long term, including financial and health concerns. If you can't be healthy doing your thing, then maybe you should try something else. Along that same vein, you need to make sure your self-compassion and self-care are firmly in place. If you're always saying "yes" to everyone else (including family), you'll soon see that you run out of "yes" for yourself. You run out of brain capacity to even know what you need to feel good, and that's no bueno.

That is very difficult for gifted and

intense people, because we struggle with not helping, not contributing, or not giving the "right" answer. We have trouble saying "no" if we're headed in the same direction. If problem-solving is one of your gifts, you may struggle with not using it—even though you *can*.

It can also be super-duper tough to let go of something that's not working. Intense people can be great at what they're interested in, and extremely difficult to sway if they feel it deserves 100% attention. An example is letting go of a product or service that hasn't done well in sales, but you believe in. Maybe the problem is the marketing, but maybe it's just not what people want!

Your intention with creating a sustainability plan should be focused on what you want your business to be in 10 years. What does your ideal day look like at that time? How do you see yourself and your clients? What will be different? What will be the same? Can you picture it vividly?

TIME TO ACT

1. Describe your plan for iteration and sustainability, based on all the work you've done so far. Show this as a mind map or flow process (or whatever makes the most sense to you), and include the extra support you'll need at each iteration. Be specific and detailed.

8
Conclusion

When I started writing this book, I wanted to give business owners a gift—the gift I want to give comes in the form of support, prodding, encouragement, information, and insight (and hopefully some tough love and humor came through, too). My hope is that you, dear reader, now have a no-nonsense guide to better understanding yourself and your business.

The Intense Entrepreneur is both a guide for entrepreneurship and a mindset for how you operate within that business. When you can focus your attention on what really matters, you'll find yourself in a whole different world. That is what I want for you because I know you've already felt isolated for too long. You no longer need to feel like you're too much because now you can bring that intensity to the table and be proud that it's your strength. You can see who you are, how you want to be perceived, and the best ways to go into the world with all your intense glory.

You now have tools for making your business phenomenal, because your business reflects who you are and how you feel about yourself. You can reach your ideal potential clients, in your most authentic voice. You have a plan of attack for sales and marketing, and you know what conditions will be ideal for collaboration. You have a very special personality, and it's made more unique by your intensities. You are a scientist and experimentation is the latest addition to your (already extensive) job description.

Take a look back and give yourself some kudos, friend! You've traveled a crazy, winding path, and it's not always fun (or easy). Always remember to give yourself heaps of self-compassion and generous self-high-fives. You're making things happen and that's something to be proud of!

Look ahead to see what's in store for you. What will you do to create the future you are envisioning? I know you will use these tools to go forward with a new mindset that will nurture your gifts.

Go back to your Chapter 1 work, and look at your sub-goals and overall goal (chief initiative). Is it still do-able? Is it challenging enough? Do you need to tweak it to make it better, bigger, or more reasonable? Stretch yourself. If it's not "close to impossible" then it can be improved upon.

Appendix A -- Resources

Book List — in no particular order
Change by Design, by Tim Brown
Presence, by Amy Cuddy
The Introvert Entrepreneur, By Beth Beulow
The 7 Habits of Highly Effective Teens, by Sean Covey
The 7 Habits for Managers, by Stephen R. Covey
Your Rainforest Mind, by Paula Prober
Quiet, by Susan Cain
Pre-Suasion, by Robert Cialdini

*The Subtle Art of Not Giving a F*ck,* by Mark Manson
Influence, by Robert Cialdini
The Fifth Discipline, by Peter Senge
Strengths Finder 2.0, by Tom Rath
Smarter Faster Better, by Charles Duhigg
The Lean Startup, by Eric Ries
Getting Naked, by Patrick Lencioni
Emotional Intelligence 2.0, by Travis Bradberry and Jean Greaves
Creating Innovators, by Tony Wagner
Disrupt You!, by Jay Samit
Bold, by Peter Diamandis
Ask, by Ryan Levesque
The E-Myth Revisited, by Michael E. Gerber
Quiet Power Strategy, by Tara Gentile
Fascinate, by Sally Hogshead
11 Rules for Creating Value in the Social Era, by Nilofer Merchant
Bright Not Broken, by Diane M. Kennedy, Rebecca S. Banks, Temple Grandin
Content Inc., by Joe Pulizzi

New Rules of Marketing and PR, by David Meerman Scott

Oversubscribed, by Daniel Priestley

The 12 Secrets of Highly Successful Women, by Gail McMeekin

Highly Intuitive People, by Heidi Sawyer

Your Rainforest Min, by Paula Prober

The Gifted Adult, by Mary-Elaine Jacobsen

Gifted Grownups, by Marylou Kelly Streznewski

Living with Intensity, by Susan Daniels and Michael M. Piechowski

Enjoying The Gift of Being Uncommon, by Willem Kuipers

Refuse to Choose, by Barbara Sher

All of the above authors probably have their own websites.

Websites for Giftedness

InterGifted, an international group supporting gifted adults www.intergifted.com

Paula Prober https://rainforestmind.wordpress.com

SENG, Supporting Emotional Needs of the Gifted www.sengifted.org
Hoagies Gifted www.hoagiesgifted.org
Gifted Development Center www.gifteddevelopment.com
Davidson Institute www.davidsongifted.org
Daimon Institute www.daimoninstitute.com
NAGC www.nagc.org

Appendix B -- Activities

The activities here correspond to the "Time to Act" section at the end of every chapter. It's the same work, just all in one place.

> **Chapter 1 Learning Objectives**
>
> 1. What are the challenges you've identified? What's holding you back in your business?
> 2. What is your Chief Initiative? Be specific.
> 3. What are the sub-goals that will help you achieve the Chief Initiative? What do you need

to accomplish that will allow you to reach the big goal?

Chapter 2 Learning Objectives

1. What are your top 10 values?
2. What was your type in the Myers-Briggs assessment? What aspects of your type resonate the most with you?
3. What was your archetype in the Fascination Advantage? List your adjectives that best describe how you do your best work.
4. Start creating a website. Use it to help you get organized. Use language from the Myers-Briggs and the Fascination Advantage to express your voice on the website, blog, and any other content creation that you work on.

Chapter 3 Learning Objectives

1. Write down your values. Yes, you did this for the last chapter, I just want you to re-

write them to highlight what you really believe in and what you're doing.

2. Now write down what you *don't* stand for. What will you not accept in your business? — what values do you reject?

3. Describe the leadership qualities you feel will make you a great leader. Show how you will put these into practice in your daily work.

Chapter 4 Learning Objectives

1. Describe, in detail, your Networking Event strategy. Include pre- during- and post-event details.

2. Describe, in detail, your Ongoing Networking strategy. Include a schedule for connection that you will commit to.

Chapter 5 Learning Objectives

1. Describe your sales strategy. Determine the products/services you will provide and their prices. Describe how you will reach people at various levels of engagement.

2. Describe your marketing strategy, based on

your values, MB, and FA. Implement it into your website, blog, and all other outreach materials.
3. Create a logic model for your business.

Input	Activities	Output	Outcome

Describe your Data collection methods (ex. google analytics, # clients, etc.), and indicators of desired outcomes (what you're actually measuring, what success means).
Commit to a regular schedule for keeping track of your measurable outcomes (put it in your calendar). Weekly? Daily? Every other day? Come up with what's relevant and tweak it if it's not giving you enough information (or too much).

Chapter 6 Learning Objectives

1. Describe your plan for creating a sense of community in for your business, including answering the following questions. What methods of connection will you use? How will you create value in your community? How will you measure success

in your community? Will you include strategic or other collaborations?

Chapter 7 Learning Objectives

1. Describe your plan for iteration and sustainability, based on all the work you've done so far. Show this as a mind map or flow process (or whatever makes the most sense to you), and include the extra support you'll need at each iteration. Be specific and detailed.

Chapter 8 Learning Objectives

1. Go back to your Chapter 1 work, and look at your sub-goals and overall goal (chief initiative). Is it still do-able? Is it challenging enough? Do you need to tweak it to make it better, bigger, or more reasonable? Stretch yourself. If it's not "close to impossible" then it can be improved upon.

Appendix C -- Lists

Values (Chapter 2)

Abundance
  Acceptance
  Accomplishment
  Accuracy
  Achievement
  Action
  Adventure
  Aesthetics
  Alignment
  Altruism
  Artistic
  Assistance
  Attainment
  Augment
  Authenticity
  Autonomy
  Awareness
  Awe
  Balance
  Beauty
  Bliss
  Boldness
  Bravery
  Calm
  Candor
  Choice
  Clarity
  Comfort
  Commitment
  Community
  Compassion
  Competition
  Completion
  Conformity

Inquisitive
Inspiration
Integration
Integrity
Intentionality
Intimacy
Intuition
Invention
Judgment
Justice
Laughter
Leadership
Learning
Love
Loyalty
Magic
Magnificence
Mastery
Movement
MysticismNature
Nurture
Openness
Orderliness
Originality
Partnership
Patience
Peacefulness
Perception
Perfection
Performance
Perseverance
Personal
Persuasion
Planning

Congruent	Playfulness
Connection	Pleasure
Contemplation	Power
Contentment	Preparation
Contribution	Privacy
Control	Process
Courage	Professionalism
Creativity	Prosperity
Dedication	Quest
Delight	Question
Dependable	Radiance
Devotion	Realization
Direct	Recognition
Discernment	Refinement
Divinity	Reflection
Drama	Relationship
Dream	Religious
Educate	Resilience
Elegance	Respect
Empathy	Responsibility
Empowerment	Reverence
Encouragement	Risk taking
Energy	Romance
Enjoyment	Safety
Enlightenment	Satisfaction
Entertainment	Security
Excellence	Self-expression
Exhilaration	Sensation
Expansion	Sensuality
Expert	Serenity
Faith	Service
Family	Sincerity
Feeling	Solitude
Flexibility	Space
Focus	Spirit

Forgiveness	Spirituality
Freedom	Spontaneity
Fun	Stimulation
Glamour	Strength
Grace	Superiority
Gratitude	Synthesis
Growth	Tenderness
Guidance	Thinking
Harmony	Thoughtfulness
Health	Thrill
Holistic	Touch
Honesty	Transformation
Honor	Trust
Hope	Truth
Humor	Understanding
Image	Uniqueness
Imagination	Unity
Improvement	Vision
Independence	Vitality
Individuality	Vulnerability
Influence	Wealth
Information	Wholeness
Ingenuity	Will

Methods of Connection — Ideas for engagement (Chapters 4, 5, and 6)

- In person, phone, or Skype (1-on-1 or in groups)
- Subscription without fees
- Subscription community with fees

- Give a lecture/talk on a stage of some sort (coffee shop to TED talk, any stage)
- Networking events (meetup, toastmasters, etc.)
- Conferences
- YouTube Video series
- Webinar
- Periscope
- Parties (networking event not specifically made for networking)
- Posters/cards on message boards
- Demonstration booth
- Facebook (personal and business)
- Twitter
- Instagram
- Other social media
- Email (not newsletter)
- Newsletters

- Book Club
- Moms group
- Courses
- Meet-ups
- Retreats
- Interviews with people you admire
- Workshops/Seminars
- Radio shows
- Podcasts
- Guest blogging on someone else's blog
- Tip sheets/worksheets/workbooks (free stuff you give away on your website)
- Other ideas?? Get creative!!

About the author

Nikki Petersen is an intense person, and has passed her intensity on to her children. They have taken that characteristic and are running hog wild with it, running through life like a bull in a china shop. She hopes they'll never stop.

Nikki is a business strategy coach, working with intense entrepreneurs and leaders. Her clients tend to be adult versions of her kids, which is why she loves them so dearly. She also hopes they will never stop pushing, asking questions, and striving to be more of what is so intensely good in this world.

www.ingramcontent.com/pod-product-compliance
Lightning Source LLC
LaVergne TN
LVHW051520070426
835507LV00023B/3219